Library of
Davidson College

Joel Oppenheimer

Poetry, the Ecology of the Soul

TALKS AND SELECTED POEMS

Edited by David Landrey and Dennis Maloney

White Pine Press

© 1983 White Pine Press
Second Edition ©1984
all rights revert to authors

Publication of this volume was made possible, in part, by a grant from the National Endowment for the Arts

Acknowledgements

Some of these poems have previously appeared in the following books and magazines: *The Dutiful Son; The Love Bit; In Time; On Occasion; The Woman Poems; Acts; Names, Dates and Places; Just Friends/Friends and Lovers; Houses; At Fifty; Bezoar; Niagara Magazine; Credences* and elsewhere. Both the author and the editors wish to thank the many editors of the books and magazines in which these poems originally appeared. For more complete information see the bibliography.

The author and the editors would also like to acknowledge a special thanks to Jim Mayer and Judy Trupin for the tiresome yet necessary work of transcribing the first draft of the talks from the original tapes. Thanks also to Robin Kay Willoughby for layout and proofing.

ISBN 0-934834-36-9

Published by
    White Pine Press
    73 Putnam Street
    Buffalo, N.Y. 14213

cover photo – Allen DeLoach

inside photos – David Landrey

CONTENTS

INTRODUCTION i

TALKS

Poetry, The Ecology of The Soul 1
Black Mountain Poets 17
The Woman Poems 30

SELECTED POEMS

from THE DUTIFUL SON
The Bath 47
The Lover 47

from THE LOVE BIT
A Flowering Avocado Tree 48
Mid-Passage 49
Mare Nostrum 49
An Undefined Tenderness 50

from IN TIME
A Note 51
Zoo Story 52
The Innocent Beasts 52
Old Story 55

from ON OCCASION
For David 57
For William Carlos Williams 57
For Matthew, Dead 60
Moratorium 61
For John & Lucy 62
The Only Anarchist General 64
Zen You 65

from THE WOMAN POEMS
Gettin' There 66
Prayer Poem II 68
The Lady of Madness 69
Mirror Poem 70
Discovery Poem 72

from **NAMES, DATES & PLACES**
A Letter to Philip 73
E.P. 1885-1972 74
Serving Notice 75
Celebrating the Peace 76

from **UNCOLLECTED POEMS**
Acts 78
Houses 81
Cacti 89
A Beginning 97
Lessons 101
Spring 105
Five Attempts At The Armenian 106
For Max 110
The Oldest 111

BIBLIOGRAPHY 112

INTRODUCTION

Joel Oppenheimer—magnificent paradox—is such testimony to, on the one hand, the principle of growth and change, and on the other hand, tenacity:

> hold on, hold on,

until the new vision comes. (see p.23 below)
Buffalo has been a recurring place for Joel to reflect upon the stages in his metamorphosis and upon the handles he has gripped. We who live here hope it has also been occasion for further growth and a tighter grip.

Although the poems contained herein evolved prior to Buffalo's becoming a large part of Joel's life, the three talks were here indeed. The first two, "Poetry, the Ecology of the Soul" and "Black Mountain Poets," were given at Buffalo State College on successive days as part of a busy poetry week in Buffalo in October 1980. The first was offered as a public lecture, the second as part of an English major seminar in the works of Oppenheimer, Olson, Creeley, Duncan, and Dorn. Also at the college those two days, Joel conducted an open workshop/gabfest and gave a reading of his poetry. Meanwhile, across town at the University, Robert Creeley (for the Gray Chair) and Robert Bertholf (for the University) were sponsoring a huge Canadian Poetry Festival. And finally, Creeley supported a fine session at Black Mountain II College, State University of New York, at which Joel reminisced about his three years at the original Black Mountain. Why—there was barely time left to catch a few innings of the World Series. The third talk, "The Woman Poems," occurred in October 1978, also at the State College, also as part of a "Black Mountain Poets" senior seminar, and provides evidence of his constancy amid change. In March 1982, Joel returned to Buffalo to give the fourth Charles Olson memorial lectures, and, although he says, "poetics isn't my strong point," we were to see still further growth and a clear vision of the craft of poetry.

I hope readers will agree that this volume reveals how utterly Joel Oppenheimer has been in contact, "whether it's angry contact or loving contact or friendly contact or hostile contact, but contact." (p.15) He has lived his culture's crisis, descended with it into Hell, and emerged with a new vision, or many new visions. Oh, he knows that there are continual descents into Hell; he has no delusions about permanently rising. What's sad is that the culture in and with which he made the descent is full of delusions, either that it can't get out or that it never descended or that it has risen into some technological beautification. Joel would assault those delusions. The same Charles Olson who spoke the words of the first paragragh (above) to Joel in a dream, a dream of Medusa, wrote his own extraordinary vision of Hell, "In Cold Hell, In Thicket," and described a condition Joel sees in our everyday life,

> All things are made bitter, words even
> are made to taste like paper.

and then adds this celestial plaint:

> In hell it is not easy
> to know the traceries, the markings
> (the canals, the pits, the mountings by which space
> declares herself, arched as she is , the sister,
> awkward stars drawn for teats to pleasure him, the
> brother
> who lies in stasis under her, at ease any monarch or a
> happy man
>
> ...
>
> How trace and arch again
> the necessary goddess?

Joel has known that bitter taste and echoes again and again that poignant question.

The talks to follow propose *poetry* as tracing and arching. Without any phony optimism he tells us, "it's possible to get through it." (p.24) Through what? Through the "gurry"? "Detritus" (p.14) and "gurry" (p.4): words of the ecological spirit and so suggestive of life's basic ironies. For "detritus" is that pile of debris that builds up as a result of our constant wearing away of our world, the annihilation of wood and oil reserves to amass piles of cream-sugar-butter-jelly-syrup-coffee containers — truly an indigestible breaking of our fast; "gurry," as Joel tells us, was that seaman Olson's word for what builds up on our hulls from doing what we must, sailing through the waters. Olson regularly quoted Heraclitus: "Man is estranged from that which he is most familiar." As Robert Duncan once observed, that may be a statement of natural condition. We may err gravely in thinking we can cure the estrangement. Oh, we're truly in "it," and we can't get finally out of "it" (do we want to?); but we don't need to thicken "it"; we *can* get *through* "it." Poetry provides the push through, as Joel says on page 33: "Something in it grabs them, but something at the same time is disturbing them. It's the fight to move past that, to break through, to get some sort of epiphany about the poem, that allows the reader to supply the same kind of energy that hopefully the poet supplied to it." No bland consolation here but, as he says at the outset, "a literal living with."

The poetry that Joel has evolved and is proposing is, as you will see, poetry of myth. Whether *The Woman Poems*, wherein there is a most direct tracing of the necessary goddess, or poems like "Lessons" and "A Beginning," wherein there is a link to historic legend, or poems like "Acts," "Houses," "Cacti," and "Spring," wherein the immediate is living myth—Joel has discovered that the myth is real. It is surely the simplest, most direct perception of "the whole life force itself" (p.5); and the one thing that simplicity cannot survive Joel reveals on page 5: "what we can't live with is duplicity." I place, then, Joel's poetic proposition in an unfolding tradition that includes not only Olson and his great spiritual father, to whom Joel is *The Dutiful Son*, William Carlos Williams, but also R.W. Emerson and Robert Duncan. In *Nature*, the piece which poses the question, "Why should not we also enjoy an original relation with the universe?" Emerson speaks of duplicity (and, by extension, of "detritus"):

> When simplicity of character and the sovereignty of ideas is broken up by the prevalence of secondary desires,—the desire of riches, of pleasure, of power, and of praise,—and *duplicity* and falsehood take place of simplicity and truth, the power over nature as an interpreter of the will is in a degree lost; new imagery ceases to be created, and old words are perverted to stand for things which are not; a paper currency is employed, when there is no bullion in the vaults.[1]

The opposite of simplicity is not complexity but duplicity. We are simple and complex at the same time, but we need not be deceptive and double-dealers. Indeed, the aim is to reconcile simple and complex in singular vision, the vision of myth. In *The Truth and Life of Myth*, Duncan issues the challenge which Joel has answered and continues to answer:

> As the story told of stars and subatomic particles and the story told of living organisms continue to reorient our possible knowledge of what is, the poetic imagination faces to challenge of finding a structure that will be the complex story of all the stories felt to be true, a myth in which something like the variety of man's experience of what is real may be contained.[2]

Note that it *does* continue. The principle is of change. But Joel has held on through an ideal simplicity. In the early 70's, as his own life changed, he heard the "necessary goddess" and poured out *The Woman Poems*, a volume that is, at once, 1) the last shout of his young voice, 2) a rendering of the aftermath of the violent 60's rebellion, and 3) a permission to move on and to expand. His work now unfolds in serene harmony with the "life force" even if he knows full-well that "it" is "a long, drawn-out losing fight."

David W. Landrey
Buffalo, New York
June, 1983

Notes:
[1] Charles Olson, *Selected Writings*, Ed, Robert Creeley (New York: New Directions, 1966) pp.182-3.
[2] Robert Duncan, *The Truth and Life of Myth:* An Essay in Essential Autobiography (Fremont, Michigan; The Sumac Press, 1968), p.12.

TALKS

Poetry, the Ecology of the Soul

I DON'T, FORTUNATELY, know how to deliver lectures. I am going to talk to you, and I hope I'm going to talk with you. I hope that I will say something of either importance or wit about poetry in that light, the ecology of the soul. I'm using the word "ecology" both hiply and loosely there, obviously, but I think it's legitimate. I think a thing we constantly get reawakened to is how much and in how many ways poetry does serve in helping us live with ourselves and where we are — and not in any despairing *giving up and living with*, but in a literal living with. It's how to live in this place where we are, on an abstract plane, i.e., life, just as we constantly have to figure out how to live *physically* where we are and with what we have been.

The composition of this talk basically is an illustration of one of the ways you write a poem. You can't sit down and make an outline for a poem. (You can, but then it turns out the poem turns out to be about something else.) What you end up doing is to allow things to come together in hopes that something will be generated by that juxtaposition. I'm sweating this out now, hoping it will happen here.

It seems to me the prime business of poets particularly — although I would assume this applies to everybody, but certainly to the poet — is to hone up and keep honed that sense we call perception, to take in what's around or inside and to learn how to live with it. A lot of people seem to get the notion with a poem, just as they do in real life, that the point is to figure out how to change it, you know, where you're living. I don't want to labor that ecology thing, but in real life the point isn't to learn how to change nature so it's good for us, but to learn how to live with it so we do O.K. and it does O.K. In the same way the function of a poem isn't to change what's around us but to change our perception of what's around, to make it easier to see in some true light or to see at all, and in that way to allow us, hopefully, to move on to something else. It's literally, I think, to give us different handles.

We're used to the definition of myth as man's attempt to understand the universe, and I think the same thing applies to poetry. I think it's why, more and more these days, at least among the poets I'm interested in reading, and I hope within myself, myth has begun to assume a larger and larger importance. We were all raised on the same scientific fact, that myth is a fairy tale, that such things don't happen, and "wasn't it cute that all those old folk believed that?" I think most of us have come to the realization that myth is quintessential fact. It's not that fairy tales are *fact*, but there's a lot there to be learned. And I always sort of feel sorry for—there are still hangovers of the rational thirties and forties who won't read their children fairy tales because they don't *mean* anything. God knows what they read them, but I've seen the kids.

I'm kind of pleased, for instance, that I took my kids to see, on a rainy Saturday, a version of "Jack and the Beanstalk" which, unbeknownst to us, was the product of some middle-European who had been soaked too heavily in Bettelheim and Freud and who had rewritten the whole thing. Both of the kids—one was twelve and one was seven-and-a-half at the time—expressed it differently, but when we walked out, essentially what they said to me was, "Boy, did that guy fuck up a perfectly good story." They were absolutely right. There were little mice that were anthropomorphic, there was a dog, who was Jack's conscience, to tell him what to do. The ogre was sort of a nice schmuck with an evil mother. That could be a perfectly good story and it might even be a useful story. This is not to put down Bettelheim or Freud that much, because, properly used, what they're doing can be useful. There's a legitimate reason for inquiry into a fairy tale like "Jack and the Beanstalk" and to debate what it might mean in terms of the consciousness of the race. Does it mean, as they think, a resolution of the Oedipal conflict by chopping down the vine? or does it mean, as I think, the separation of the id, the ego, and the super-ego, and the consequential need for Momma to convince you that the super-ego is bad? As soon as I had that realization I realized why I had always sort of liked ogres. I really flashed back to being six months old and already being trained that all those evil, hungry impulses of mine had to be curbed. Those things are there in our heads and they're more and more useful to know about. But leave the myth, the fairy tale, alone, while you're studying.

Years ago I was reading a book on the archeology of Western Europe by a man named Oakeshott, an Englishman, who had started out from weaponry. He was a specialist in Medieval weapons and he had sort of extended himself backward in time. It was a book concerning recent finds of weapons of prehistoric Western European people, i.e., pre-written history. He succeeded not only in giving me the best prehistory of Western Europe I had seen, but in validating, as he himself pointed out, a great deal of the early "mythic" writings. He used as an example his teacher reading, when he was in sixth or seventh grade, a passage from Beowulf describing a helmet in great detail, with little golden pigs leaping over the ears, and a deer in full flight across the forehead, and so forth. The teacher talked about what a wonderful "imagination" those funny old people had. Then Oakeshott says, "Turn to plate two." You find a helmet which was dredged up from the Thames dated 700 A.D., around the time Beowulf was thought to have been written, and it's that helmet. The pigs are there and the deer is there and they *did* it. That's what I'm saying to you, that I think now we have the validation that those poets weren't crazy. They were writing about real things and they had real perceptions and useful perceptions. So I use that for a validation for my own crazy perceptions, not that that means that every perception I have is accurate, but that I've discovered that it's at least as accurate as NASA's evaluation of the moon rock data and maybe more so. I would like to think certainly a lot more useful. I'm positing as a general rule that poetry's not only the ecology of the soul, but it's the ecology of what we might call the total soul, that universal consciousness. I liked very much that yesterday one of the Canadian "sound" poets said "There is no unconscious," and I've decided to adopt that position also. We may not know it, but it's all there, and it's stupid to break it up into unconscious, subconscious, conscious. It's all there and it's all useful—if we tap into it.

Poetry is becoming more and more useful today because poets are among the few people who are intent—not all poets, but some poets—on using the language. Most language around you today condemns itself simply by what it says, not to mention how it says it. The fact is that most of our rulers and our leaders are illiterate as you can plainly hear by listening to them talk. When they are trying to be literate they are lying, generally, as you can plainly see by reading the words they say (not to mention the actions that follow). Forget that, because all of us do that, but at least some of us talk true and then don't deliver; they're talking false and still not delivering.

I'm not going to turn this into a reading, I promise, but even lecturers use examples once in a while. I'm going to use a poem as an example. It happens to be a poem of mine; it's from a series which utilizes both my own, i.e. my invented, poems, and found poems, taken from places that seem to me to say something, and some of them combine both techniques. Right now I want to read one which is almost word for word, "found." I have the original clipping from whence it comes at home. I haven't put anything in a new order in this. I believe it is word for word, with a possible alteration in some of the punctuation where it may have been broken into separate sentences while I've made it a list. But I have not changed any words, any meanings. It's from a series called *At Fifty:*

> they set up headquarters
> registered the prospectors
> declared the site closed
> to any others
> vaccinated the colony
> against yellow fever and meningitis
> banned women and alcohol
> announced that anyone
> firing a weapon
> would be expelled
> set up a loudspeaker
> to play country music
> during off hours
> and the national anthem
> at morning and evening
> flag raising and lowering
>
> each night soft-core
> pornographic films
> are shown on the airstrip

Now you know there's no way I could make that up, or if I did it would just be cute, but these people actually did this. This is the new gold rush in Brazil. They did it and the *Times* wrote it. I don't want to put on airs, but as far as I know I'm the only one who saw what that was saying. Now you see it too, that incredible *list*. I love "banned women and alcohol"; really, it's real life. The juxtapositions and that incredible ending—the soft core porn. I have nothing against soft core pornography. I love looking at naked women. But my God, it's there, it's there in the words, what they are saying! A lot of these new poems come from the *Times* science section or the *Times* editorials. I hate to pick on them, but I read them every day, and they pretend to be the newspaper of record and one of our literate voices, so why not.

We live in an age when the language is constantly being, to use an Olsonian term, gurried, covered with gurry. I looked that up once. I think it's the muck that collects on a ship's hull and that has to be scraped off. Just by virtue of the fact that the ship's doing what it should, which is sail through water, it picks up gurry. So we have to cut through the gurry, not change the world, but cut through the gurry.

Another example, certainly, to get back to that notion of ecology, living in balance, is that it takes some people a long time to learn that being in love with someone doesn't mean that you're supposed to change them; it means that you're supposed to learn to live with them, that you want to learn to live with them because you love them. Well, I would like to propose that that's what the poets I care about are doing and are helping the rest of us do, that having made a decision that willy-nilly we're stuck where we are, doing what we're doing and surrounded with what we are surrounded by, we better try to understand it and learn how to live with it.

I'm not talking about putting up with that which can be changed. Obviously, I'm talking about the whole life force itself, as opposed to what stops us from living. What are those things that won't let us live, won't let us reach out to each other, won't let us use the world in the best sense, which is to use it without using it up. I think that's one of the proper functions of a poem these days, just as, when Horace lived in Rome, because it was a different world, Horace made a decision that the function of a poem was to educate, hence didactic poetry, poetry which teaches, which lectures, all that dreadful stuff which we can't live with now because we're in a different place. Still, once you get that notion past you, then you can read it. But reading it the first time you say "My God, what is this man doing?" What he was doing was responding to the needs of his time. I think we have to respond to the needs of our time. That's clear in every other field, so I don't see why it shouldn't be in art, especially since we know that the artists generally have been the ones first and most responsive to the needs of their time. That quick response is why everyone else gets upset, exactly why everyone else gets upset, especially those in a position of authority. They're living off, they're making a profit off, the way things are. So naturally if Horace, then, was lecturing on morality, or someone today is screaming about immorality (even in immoral terms, as some of us have been known to do) then of course those who have a vested interest in keeping things the way they are will get upset. Ergo, the *New York Times* "Book Review," and what they tell us to read.

To bounce back, there was an item on the front page of today's paper about a Columbus television station which asked people if they would vote for Nixon if he were running today, and sixty-five percent said yes! I got furious. This man had made a career out of preaching morality and was himself immoral—not because he cursed on the tapes; I curse all the time and I spend half my time telling my children that just because I curse doesn't mean they have to, and there are better ways to say things, and there's appropriate language, etc., etc. and I'm also a charter member of a society called Maledicta which devotes itself to the study of cursing. I was mad not because Nixon cursed, and certainly not that he cursed in private, but that he cursed in private and presented a different face in public. If he had stood up and run for office on the grounds that "the rest of them are shitheads, and I know what the fuck to do about it," we could live with that. What we can't live with is duplicity.

Confucius has several chapters on what happens when a government lies to the people, and how you tell whether, in fact, the society is operating properly. The first fact always is, do the words mean what they say? I think that poets in general, these days, have the function of making the words mean what they say, of cleaning up the language. There have, of course, always been poets who have just played with the language, sometimes well and sometimes badly. Sometimes they played in the service of this cleaning up, and sometimes they just muddied the issue. It could be "muddled" too, as in a beginning, a muddle, and an end. That's where we are now I think; I mean, where I am. I'm in the muddle, I'll get to the end eventually. Okay: I don't want to take away that function of playing with the language, even if it sometimes muddies or muddles things. I certainly don't want to take away the "beautiful poem" because that, too, has a function. But I'm talking now about something that seems to me imperative to keep an eye on, which is this act of cleaning the language, of making sure that the words say what they mean, that we're seeing truly, that we're talking like our old friend, Red Jacket, with a straight tongue. The image of the forked tongue is a very powerful one.

We live in a society where the forked tongue has become the way of life. I know a lot of you are taking disciplines where you'll be expected to use a forked tongue: sociologists who will be expected, who will be given bad grades, if you don't write in sociological jargon, or education majors who will be given bad grades if you don't write in educational jargon, etc., etc., etc. Even, God forbid, though I can't believe it with these splendid people here, that you could be taught to write in English pedagogical jargon. But why does this jargon exist? The notion was that it might make those disciplines, the communication of those disciplines more precise. It pretty rapidly turned, as it always does when you set up a jargon, into a secret code. If you pay your dues, and talk the secret language, and nobody else can understand you, then you're O.K. God forbid, for instance, a child psychologist should write a report about a child that one of the parents might understand. That would blow the whole gig, right? So you spend four years in a discipline learning to write a language which *lies.* I'm not blaming Buffalo State; it inherited a condition from a society which wanted that condition. It's doing what it's expected to do. Fortunately, in every college and university, there are always a couple of guys who say, "Yeah, hey, these are the rules, but let me tell you how to really write." You know, *how to tell the truth,* so if you write a love letter, which the society will still allow us to write, maybe you can tell the truth in that—maybe. Or if you write a letter to the milkman about how much to deliver, he'll be able to understand how much to deliver. The rest of the time you'll have to use the jargon because there's no way to stop it. I'd like to say these are trying times, but I suspect that all times are trying. That's what the game is about; it comes with the territory. All you can keep doing is trying—during the trying times.

I had intended for this to flow gracefully and naturally into some sort of interchange, to use a jargon term. What I mean is, as I said at the beginning, I don't conceive of myself as a lecturer. And I have all this to share with you and you have all that to share with me. What I would really like is if somebody wants to either respond to something I've been saying or to open up some of it or ask a question or a statement. Anything short of throwing something; I don't move too well anymore.

CLASS: Pound, I think it was, in *The ABC of Reading*, said that you can judge a society by its literature, and that when the poetry and the language suffer, so does the society, and to mark the decline of society, so I guess you would have to say we've been declining for like 2000 years.

J.O.: Well, not necessarily.

CLASS: I meant, in your terms, in what you said earlier about constantly trying to clean up the language, but it comes with the territory.

J.O.: Well, it has to be done over and over again. The reason I said, "not necessarily" is because I don't care to list the poets who have written in the last 2000 years and rank them. I'm delighted that if I'd lived 3200 years ago I could have heard Homer, and if I'd lived 2500 years ago I could have heard Sappho, and if I'd lived 600 years ago I could have heard Chaucer, and so on down the line. There was always somebody, and with them, a couple of other people. I do think the problem is getting harder because now you have to deal with world-wide communication where the possibilities escalate for the dissemination of the lies. I don't know how you people would answer this question, but every once in a while I think about what would happen if I had to flee the United States. Maybe it's just that I'm old and tired and bitter, but I can't think of any place to flee. Every place I know of is just as bad or just as good. The only difference is that here I can eat the food that I'm used to eating. If I fled to some country that lived on rice and beans or some country that lived on seafood, I'd be eating a diet that I wasn't that used to, and I'd have to retrain myself. The condition has changed from when you could go to a new place and make a new language.

I don't think that anyone denies now that most governments are the same, by and large, in terms of what they're trying to accomplish and what they're trying to do with the society and what they would do if they controlled the would. Even the ones that we think of as diametrically opposed, well, the assumption is—I mean Lenin never made any bones about it—that things would change once everybody understood the way things had to be. That's essentially what the Americans have been saying: once everybody understands how to vote in a free election it'll all be perfect, i.e., American. And Lenin was saying once everybody understands that all things have to be shared among all people, everything will be perfect, i.e., Russian. So they're saying exactly the same thing, really, but it's more than that. It's that what the world-wide communication net allows, as all of you must have noticed, is the immediate export of the least common denominator, over and over again. Whether we're talking about McDonald burgers in the middle of Paris getting rated, I guess, on one pickle, two pickles, or three pickles, or the export of disco music everywhere; whatever level we're talking at it's the stuff that's the easiest, the stuff that no one needs to worry about and very few get offended by, that gets exported. When obviously what ought to get exported is the thorniest, the stuff that offends the most people, simply because we ought to have learned in these hundred thousand or two hundred thousand years that that's the stuff that counts. I hate to say it, but I feel like what my mother used to say when she was putting the iodine on is really humanly true, "It don't help unless it hurts." Maybe that's where we have to get to, that unless it hurts it's no good. The stuff that don't hurt is just going to screw us up in the end.

CLASS: The problem with that is that you can't sell pain very well.

J.O.: I know you can't, but if you take everything else off the market by subtle sabotage...; I loved those people that walked around for years telling secretaries in big offices, just quietly mentioning that (this was sort of a ring of underground messengers) "The green light in Xerox machines makes you sterile." For a long time it worked. Secretaries "preferred" not to use the Xerox machine. Or—I don't know if it got up to Buffalo but it sure swept through the third grade in New York about five years ago—that Bubble-Yum was made from spider legs. Sales just disappeared in New York City, and Bubble-Yum had to mount this enormous campaign to convince the kids that it was O.K. to chew. Well, everybody knows it's not O.K. to chew Bubble-Yum. Even the kids know it, that's why they want to chew it.

I have the feeling that there are some people here who are going to walk out and say, "Jesus, if that's what a poem is about, I ain't never reading one." Remember I said poems play also, which somebody said was what distinguishes man from the beasts, that human beings play. Certainly poems play with the language; that's another thing that offends people, that they're in some way not serious. It's curious, for example that the *Village Voice* pays me twice as much for a prose piece about the World Series as for a poem. It's just never entered their consciousness that the poem might be worth more. They take it for granted that it's worth less. Another interesting point, the National Endowment on the Arts Grants to working artists have a maximum of ten thousand dollars. The National Endowment on the Humanities Grants, to people who write *about* artists, run from twenty-three to thirty-five thousand dollars a year. These are funny little anomalies we learn to live with, because we all know that poets aren't serious, so don't give them a lot of money. They'll only waste it, put it in their mouths or something.

CLASS: Is that perhaps why so many modern poets seem to get hold of propaganda or causes? There are some who are anti-war and still on that bandwagon and write propaganda and try to pass it off as poetry. It's embarrassing.

J.O.: Well, as any of us discovers quite early in the game, propaganda and poetry don't mix. I've written some "agit-prop" poems. I did them during the height of the anti-Vietnam war movement for readings at Central Park, or Loeb student center, or what have you. I wrote them differently from other poems because I was trying literally to convince an audience of something, or to support that audience in its conviction. I certainly didn't write them for the reasons I would normally write a poem.

But what is one to do if one feels strongly about some great issue? One wants to do what one can, and what if what one can do is write? Then one writes "agit-prop." Now, one hopes that one has the good sense to say, "Oh, this one is agit-prop, and this other one is a poem, and I will read this one when I'm talking to a hundred thousand people at Central Park Sheep Meadow, and this other I will cause to get distributed to the fifty people who want to read a poem." One hopes that one has enough sense, as I say. I suspect that what's offending you, and properly, is the people who can't distinguish between the two. I think that only happens to the good poets for a short while. I think all of a sudden they snap out of it and say, "Hey, wait a minute, this is rhetoric, and it has a place, but the place isn't where I thought it was." In effect you relegate those pieces to doing what they're meant to do, which is to move people.

The "real" poems move people, too, but in a much different way. Poems don't move people in groups of ten thousand or a hundred thousand or five hundred. By and large, poems move individuals, alone in their rooms at night, or on a grassy knoll on a sunny afternoon. That's when poems work. A woman friend of mine who has read as well and as widely as anyone I know, credits a lifetime habit of two-hour baths. She gets in the tub with a bunch of books and she soaks and she reads, and when she comes out the world has changed a little, or she has, but something's different. She has built up as good a reading and as good an understanding that way as anyone I know. But that's how poems work. It's another problem, it's a reason why, for instance, books of poems sell five hundred copies, two thousand copies; once in awhile, astonishingly, five thousand copies, and then usually for the wrong reason—because they're "dirty," or they're outrageous. They may even be good, too, but people aren't buying them because they're good.

CLASS: In the same direction as the last question but from a different point: is there any danger in, say, reading or writing a poem that is too plainly and simply written or too convoluted and obscurely written? Is one worse? Could one be read too superficially if it's too clearly written.?

J.O.: Sure, but you can't worry about those dangers. If you write a poem that you believe says what you mean it to say, but it's "too" complex, then you can't sit down and say, "I'll only reach twelve people with this poem," because to change it to reach twelve hundred might mean saying it differently in a way you didn't want to say it. Conversely, if you come on a perception so simple, so clear to you, that it seems like nothing, like many people will just slide over it without getting it, again you can't worry; you've said it as well as you can. In those magic instances where you write a poem that says what you want it to say and it's also accessible to just the right number of people, whatever that number is, then the muse has smiled upon you. I think you can worry, are you saying what you mean to say and are you saying it as best as it can be said?

I'm not saying "just write it down and that's it"; obviously you have to pay attention to what you've said and how you've said it. But once you read that poem and the hair on the back of your neck stands up, then all you can do is hope that there's an audience out there somewhere that can respond the same way. It can be two and it can be two thousand. Maybe in some perfect world it can even be two million. You can't tailor it to reach; then you're doing exactly that lowest common denominator thing. You're saying, "Well, if I tinker with it a little, and I paint it red over here, maybe some more people will like it." You do what you can. I've written both kinds—ones that have been so simple that me and two other people are the only ones who understand that they're really terribly profound and ones that are so complex that only me and two other people understand that they're really very simple. I like to think that in both of those cases I was right. Of course being right doesn't mean that you win the election.

CLASS: As you said in *Houses*, it's clear you've changed. I wonder what changes you perceive to have occurred in your own poetry because the gurry has built up thicker.

J.O.: I think I've gotten back to a much simpler line structure. For a long while, certainly in the last twenty years, I've written in what I call a discursive voice. I talk around things and about them, and I tell stories in the middle of the poem. I'm always willing to throw in a funny line or an anecdote if I think it's really part of it. That all got thick and complex in books like *On Occasion* and *In Time*, and then in *The Woman Poems* the line got even more intense, that long line, that packed line. Now I've moved back to a quieter, slower line. Let me see if there's one of these that works that way. Here's a street scene from Greenwich Village:

>   seven-thirty in the morning
>   couple in shiny english boots
>   whipcord jodhpurs riding caps
>   blue broadcloth shirts whips
>   walking down hudson there
>   are no stables that way

Or, here, I have a funny poem I would like to read since the World Series ended last night:

> eleven years ago
> i stopped making love
> to watch cleon jones
> put the team ahead
> in a crucial game
>
> stopped the act of love
> to watch baseball
> on television
> a ballclub in
> a pennant race
>
> not important except
> to remember committing
> this act life vs art
> art vs art culture vs
> the individual whatever
>
> eleven years later
> there is always something
> embarrassing to remember
> something we did that was
> shameful ridiculous and
> shameful something
> to wish undone
>
> but that marriage is gone
> and the team won the pennant

CLASS: Your imagining your hair standing on end, the idea of the sensation the poem creates, brings me to something I've been thinking a lot about lately, the way the tears differ from each other in their quality or their authenticity or what causes them and the depth of magic that various things can evoke. You mention one of the poet's functions is to clean up the language, and yet certain things go with the territory. I'm just wondering, in a culture in which, seemingly, industries, commercial advertisers have a vested interest in making the consumer progressively insecure and increasing the feeling that we have a right, everybody has a right, to an almost constantly magical life or life isn't worth living, that there's a kind of superficial magic coming over the verbal cliches created by the media that makes the territory so very difficult that I wonder to what extent can the language can be cleaned up at all and and for how many people?

J.O.: That's a very serious problem. All I know is I've got to keep trying. What you say may very well be true, that it's gone too far. The evidence is in, forget the cultural implications of a televised world, forget that kind of pressure. Just look at the studies which seem to be done in enough depth and enough breadth to be acceptable scientifically about what physically, physiologically, the act of watching television does to people: the fact that it literally turns off two-thirds of the brain; the fact that the use of television as a teaching tool is increasing just as the data is mounting almost undeniably, as far as I can tell, that it is impossible to learn from television. The brain literally, physiologically, cannot receive material that comes from those little dots on a cathode-ray tube. Parts of the brain shut off, and you don't get information that way. Yet we live in a world where every second-rate teacher, which means at this point a huge percentage of them, wants nothing more than that screen next to him or her so that they will be relieved of demonstrating their own ignorance and insecurity. There are times when I know we can't win, but then I think of Paul Goodman's lovely line that "In many ways the best fight is the long, drawn-out losing fight." You know if you win too quick it's not satisfying, and certainly if you lose too quick, that ain't nothing. If you win after a long fight, you really feel sort of vaguely bad about it, like the fight was so good, the process was so good and you ended up the winner and somehow it's empty. But if you lose in a long, drawn-out, hard fight, then you really got something. You know you did your best, you didn't waste your time. Maybe that's what I'm engaged in, and maybe that's what I'm asking everybody to do. Maybe that sounds dumb, but on the other hand, maybe if enough people go into it thinking it may be a long, drawn-out losing fight, maybe we change things a little.

CLASS: That's very heroic. One thing we learned from the three Viking presentations we just had here in Buffalo was that the Vikings believed the world was going to end, y'know, Twilight of the Gods, but that didn't mean they should stop fighting. They had to keep those ice giants and the wolves away from the door.

J.O.: You know, when you first said, "that's very heroic," I thought, "Oh, God, here it comes," but that ends up one of the sweetest things anyone's ever said to me, in that reference. Sure, they knew that the world was an alien, hostile place that they had to learn to live with or they would die, and that what they had to try and change for their own needs they would try and change, but that it was a long, drawn-out losing fight. Sure, the Vikings believed—as those of you who paid attention to that know—that what counted was, did you go down bravely in that fight? Did you go down bravely? Did you behave the way a Viking should behave, did you die well? Well, especially in this age of instant gratification, it's hard to tell people that what they ought to be looking for are ways to fight the good fight and die well. Not many people are going to believe you. Maybe it doesn't take that many. Maybe only a few have to be willing to do that to turn things around at least a little bit. Sure, it's heroic and foolish, but then the best poems always are—both—heroic and foolish. It's an old truth that nobody wants to hear anymore, but the world is not essentially a happy place with a couple of sad spots. It's essentially a sad place with a few happy spots: once in awhile you're up, and that's what makes being up wonderful.

I could go back to my favorite referent, the Yankee fans who have been so spoiled by almost incessant winning that not only does losing become a verdict from heaven, but it means they deny anything else exists. I know Yankee fans who didn't watch a single inning of the World Series simply because if the Yankees weren't in it, it wasn't a World Series. That's a kind of strange view of the universe, but that comes when you think that the world is a happy place. Then you have to say it doesn't exist when it gets sad. If you know the world is a sad place, then the good things are really good. No Yankee fan has ever in his life, and don't laugh when I say this even though it's funny, but no Yankee fan in his life has ever known the joy I felt either as a Dodger fan in '55 or a Mets fan in '69. There's no way that they could, even though they had hours, endless hours of happy hours, watching a superb ball team win and win and win. Nothing could compare.

It had occurred to me a while back that I had grown up in a terribly repressed era. I was born in 1930, so I came of sexual age in the forties. I mean repressed on all levels, too. Girlie magazines for fifteen-year-old boys were either the underwear section of the Sears catalogue, or if you lived near New York City, the lingerie ads in the *Times* Sunday Magazine. The perceived wisdom was that people who had been married more than six or eight weeks weren't getting it on more than once or twice a month. But it occurred to me yesterday that now that we're beginning to get some results in from the sexual revolution, people weren't noticeably less happy about sexual matters than then now. There was a brief flurry when people seemed happier, but it didn't last long. People are just as unhappy now, sexually, as they were then, even though they're all, if I am to believe the reports, screwing madly six times a night, probably with twelve different partners. And none of the partners has hair curlers in, or torn flannel nightgowns, male or female. Well, some of the males may.

I laugh when corporations announce that they're going to do one of those two-week retreats where the top execs go someplace and rethink what's happening. Maybe the world needs that, maybe we ought to sit down for two weeks in some quiet place and rethink what's been going on, and say, "Hey, is it really 'better'? is it demonstrably worse? is it the same?" If it's the same, maybe we ought to consider going back some distance since it certainly was less complicated before. If it's the same maybe we should get rid of some of the complications.

Example: is there a Friendly's in Buffalo? Have any of you ever walked into Friendly's at a slow time and ordered? It takes Friendly's four times longer to deliver an order than my inefficient greasy spoon, where, when there's nobody there and you walk in, Paul says, "Oh, a hamburger? coming right up," and just slaps it on. In Friendly's they've got the machine set up so it will service sixty-three hamburgers a minute, and so, if there's only one hamburger, it takes the same time as the sixty-three. So what I'm saying is, maybe we ought to think about—does fast food really make it faster? Maybe we oughta go back to slow food because it takes exactly the same amount of time, and it tastes better, but we'll forget that.

I'll pick on Friendly's again, about another thing that bugs me—I lived around the corner from a Friendly's in Oneonta for a month last summer with my kids, and we had a lot of breakfasts in there. I always found it astonishing that when you walked into an empty Friendly's at 11:01 in the morning, they could not cook breakfast for you. Again, Paul in the greasy spoon, at the height of the lunch hour, seems to have no problem scrambling some eggs, along with making the hot plates and the sandwiches and everything else. These are silly examples; unfortunately they are the stuff we have to live with, that we've done to ourselves, that we've let them do to us.

I did an article up in Maine a couple of summers ago, on Mount Desert Island, one of God's gifts to us, in Bar Harbor, one of mankind's gifts to us. It suddenly occurred to me that in order to eat in Bar Harbor, you have to have sharp fingernails and a table large enough to accumulate this mass of detritus which grows because everything is given to you wrapped up. Various industries have gotten laws passed that forbid the placing of cream in pitchers, or sugar in bowls, or butter in a dish. Everything has to come in either paper or plastic or cellulose so that things get used up. Even the maple syrup comes in little, impossible-to-open, packets which get all over your fingers instead of the waffles. When you say something about it, they say, well, it's cheaper. It can't be cheaper! They say it's more efficient. It can't be more efficient! Once in awhile they tell a little bit of the truth. They say it has a longer shelf life. Well, that's their problem, not mine, and I really don't want to hear about it. I mean, I don't expect a cow to come to the table, but I would rather not know that I'm drinking some cream that came out of some cow seven years ago and has this wonderful shelf life.

CLASS: In Britain an efficiency expert found out that a little brewery that used a horse to deliver the real ale was more efficient...

J.O.: There was a report in the *Times* a couple of weeks ago about some of those "idealistic hippies" that moved up to Vermont and New Hampshire in the sixties and now have gotten their acts together and have working farms going. The supermarkets have discovered they can buy good vegetables cheaper from them, even though they're using "organic growing methods," non-chemical methods, than they can on the shit that's turned out on that assembly farm in California, where they put the tomatoes together with an inedible skin and a square shape, so they ship easy. I got some peaches this summer from the supermarket that looked gorgeous. They never got ripe! They rotted before they ripened. It was incredible. They sat there for two weeks looking beautiful, and then one day they were rotten. At no point had they ever been soft enough to eat. It's a triumph of modern engineering.

The article said essentially that these people, who are doing everything wrong, were able to supply the product cheaper and better than the efficient way. I think that shows all over. My God, have any of you ever thought about how simple it used to be to wash your hands after you peed? You turned a little knob and water came out. If it was too cold you turned the other one and it came out. If they were coming out too hard you loosened or tightened them a little, and they came out softer. If a leak developed you unscrewed—and I'm not mechanical—but I could do it!—you unscrewed the top and you took out a little flat thing and you took it to the hardware man. Some people knew the names of what to ask for, but I used to take it to the hardware man. "Could I have one of these?" He gave it to me and I put it back in and turned it on and it ran without dripping. Now, they have some goddam machine that you sort of tug a number of ways and finally water comes out, either too hard to put your hands under or not hard enough to get any water. It's never possible to control the temperature. And the little sign says, "This is our most modern efficient faucet." And the world goes on. On and on—in every area like this. Like I said—it's silly. I shouldn't at an important place like this and with an important series like this lecture series be talking about such things because they're not "meaningful." Except it happens to be what we live with every day and it is, in its own obvious way, an absolute representation of what's happening in the world: nothing works anymore. What does work, we don't want or can't use or have to force ourselves to figure out how to use. The things that we really do want are harder and harder to find, like a human ear to listen to our voice or a human voice for our ear to listen to or, God forbid, a little patch of skin to touch or be touched by.

What a depressing note that was. Can someone find something cheerful?

CLASS: Isn't what you're hungering for? A little tender loving care?

J.O.: No, because that's too easy an answer. Of course it isn't a little T.L.C.. Maybe what I'm hungering for is those touches and those voices and some honest fights, where you know what it is you're lashing out against, and you know what it is that's hitting you. I'm not asking for some simple fairyland world. I'm asking for a world where you can feel like you're a human being, where you can feel like there is human contact, whether it's angry contact or loving contact or friendly contact or hostile contact, but contact, where there's a possibility of learning something about the world you live in, the place you're at, what you yourself are, instead of continually running from any of those knowledges because they hurt or because it takes time or trouble.

CLASS: I think you've lived up to your goal of sensitizing us to things that we can change and things that we can't change. Or to quote Chaucer, "You've taught us how to maken the vertue of necesitee."

J.O.: Thank you. That was going to be my alternate title for the lecture.

Keep up the fight. Or, as I said to an old friend, Sam Abrams, in Rochester, "Keep fighting the good fight, Sam." He said, "I'm looking for the people you surrender to." See you again.

Black Mountain Poets

CLASS: Where did you get this Mother theory?
J.O.: From my racial memory. From Mother. Well, actually, from both of those, plus the fact that, to a certain extent, it resurfaced generally. Robert Bly had written a seminal essay called, "I Came Out of the Mother Naked." It dealt with the re-emergence of the Mother Goddess; he wrote it in maybe '71 or '72. In fact, Bly has been running every year now, since then, seminars in the summer on what he calls, "The New Father," which attempt—as far as I know since I've never been to any of them; I've talked to a couple of people who have been there—to discuss in both real and mythological terms The New Man, in terms of the Mother Goddess, like where, in fact, men, not the general term "men," but specifically men, ought to be, or are, with what he takes to be the re-emergence of the Mother Goddess on the scene. I read *The Woman Poems* at a small college in New Hampshire shortly after they were finished, and some dewy-eyed lad in the front row said, "You sound like you've discovered a new religion," and I said, "or been converted to a very old one." In that sense it's an homage to some feelings that run very deep in me, and I think in everyone, and something that, as Bly talks a great deal about, has been severely repressed, not only the knowledge of the Great Mother, to begin with, and not only the political implications—the fact that the church found it necessary to destroy, literally, the old religion. All our stories about witches come from that repression, from the fact that there was a religion practiced that women were very deeply involved in, and then the church found it necessary, as it moved particularly into Western Europe and the British Isles, to suppress this and began building up tales about these horrid old crones who did terrible things to people. And again, as Bly points out in his essay, we lose by it. We are less people by not feeling this presence.

It also happened to happen at a time when I was going through a severe re-examination, to use nice words. My second marriage had suddenly crashed; it was five years of unremitting hell, and I was in a position of trying to figure out why, and how, and where I was in it; and it was a good time to think about what I was as a person, and as a man, in terms of that eternal love-hate relationship between men and women; and so it all sort of came together. Now I had been at large poetry conference with Bly, about six months before, or a year before these poems came pouring out, and he had talked a little bit about the Mother, and there's no doubt in my mind that that triggered everything, but what got triggered was a lot of material that was there already. It just sort of served as a crystallization point, a catalyst, to get things rolling. I've said somewhere that I had the choice between sitting down and reading all the material, or writing the poems, and I chose to write the poems rather than read the material.

As a matter of fact, I've told you, I think, that Bob Bertholf, who is now over at the library at UB and was then teaching at Kent State, was horrified to discover, or bemused is a better word, that I had never read the key text about the Mother Goddess, which is a book called *The Great Mother*, by Erich Neumann, who was a disciple of Carl Gustav Jung. It's a wonderful book about what is known, what is surmised, about the religion of the Great Mother, and so, when he discovered that I hadn't done this, he promptly went out and bought me a copy, and I dutifully read the first, the introductory, chapter and the first two chapters, and then it sort of ground down, and I spilled some coffee on it, and, you know, it's on my shelf, and I look at it every once in a while. There's a wonderful picture of a Tibetan goddess named Dancing Mother, named Tara, who may be the most beautiful woman I've ever seen in my life, so every once in a while I open up the back to the illustrations and look at Tara, and wonder where she is these days, and how she's getting on.

I know that the impulse is, again and again—we keep coming back to this—to want to be given solid and easy answers, like this was something planned, and I got to it because of a, b, and c, and having gotten to it, I then moved on to d, e, and f. But I'm afraid that ain't the way it works. It, as I say, came bubbling out. It was the first writing I had done in perhaps fifteen years where I literally felt the presence of the Muse while I wrote. That's not discounting the work in between, but just to say that you learn once you commit yourself to writing, you learn that the Muse isn't always going to be there, and that a lot of the time you're writing simply because you keep calling yourself a writer, and that's what you do. I was blessed—I realize how romantic and corny this sounds, but I mean it—I was blessed; she came back and hung around the house for three months. The first seven poems in *The Woman Poems*, not counting the first two or three, which were written earlier—and it occurred to me when I had the body finished that they belonged in there, and if I'd had any control over the design of the book, I would have made it clearer that they are prefatory poems, literally—but the first seven poems of the book proper were written in three days, and the rest sort of just came barreling and bucketing along. And in fact, there are poems in it for which I just jotted down notes, not about the poems, but just titles. I'd be working on something, and it would occur to me that I'd have to write a poem about so-and-so, and I would write a note with just a title, and maybe three weeks later, look at the note and say, "oh yeah," and the poem would just be there. Now that's not my normal process of writing; it is kind of wonderful and magical, and I'm delighted it happened. As I was saying before—I guess some of you might have heard—he asked about the change in voice between *The Woman Poems* and things like *Houses* and *Cacti*. And I said that I had originally thought, when I worked on them, that they were really a breakthough in voice, in the way I was saying things, and it wasn't until later, until two or three years later, it began to dawn on me that what that voice really was was the culmination of the voice I had used all along, sort of the last shout, and having said that, having done that, then about two years later, the voice changed, very dramatically for me, that is, it was a big wrench. I wrote a short poem that was totally different from that voice, and everything since then, really, has flowed from that one short poem in terms of how I see constructing a poem. Now once in a while, because it's something I know how to do, I go back to that other voice, but I go back to it in the way you do use a tool you know how to use, because it works for a particular situation.

CLASS: What poem was that?

J.O.: You don't know it. You may have heard it, but you don't know it. This is in small collection that the printer I mentioned last night, Walter Hamady, has, and which will eventually come out. The book is called *Del Quien Lo Tomo*, which means roughly, "from him who took it," and it's an homage both to William Carlos Williams, one of whose earliest books was called *Al Que Quiere*, "to him who wishes it," or "to him who wants it," and to Paul Blackburn. Anyhow, the book ends—it's a short sequence of poems—and it ends with this poem, "Autumn":

>   the weather
>   moving
>   one side of the continent
>   to the other
>
>   in the park
>   one relaxed arm
>   drapes easily
>   over her friend's arm
>
>   movement
>   touch
>   how they work
>
>   all I know
>   the body
>   the poem

Now what was happening in terms of form there was simply a much greater compression in the kind of discursiveness, the kind of talking about things that goes on in *The Woman Poems*. In the syntax it's compressed, and yet I'm still trying to get as much in, I'm not trying to avoid talking *about*; when I sat down to write this poem, I knew that I wanted to talk *about* that woman in the park, the way she was sitting. Well, in *The Woman Poems*, that might have turned into eight or ten lines, with an extended description of how she was sitting, and why it was important to me, etc., etc.; and here it becomes, "in the park/ one relaxed arm/ drapes easily/ over her friend's arm." And I was kind of startled by how hard it was to do that, to get things that simple. I hope that it's working for you the way it worked for me, seeing her. But the notion was—I mean after all it literally was a glimpse, a glance, as I walked by this park near my house, with these weather changes going on, with fall coming on, and just seeing this couple sitting there, and the way the arm was. So I was trying to get both that sense that Williams talks about of the brush stroke of Chinese painting, the quick stroke which, if correct, stays, if not, you throw away the drawing, because you can't work over wet rice paper, so you just learn to do the strokes. So I was trying to do that stroke and at the same time carry all that that glimpse was. Since it was only a glimpse, obviously I couldn't write three pages about it.

And a compression in the syntax of "movement/ touch/ how they work." It was the poem where finally, although there probably are earlier ones, I've never checked, but this is the one where I was conscious that I'd finally figured out how to write a poem without the interference of punctuation, and yet have it be readable in syntactical terms. I have nothing against punctuation, as I have nothing against capitals, but I do think they intrude on your reading. I think they make you do certain things outside the reading. And obviously, if I'm reading a report about the World Series in *The Buffalo Evening News* or *The New York Times*, or whatever, I want there to be punctuation so I can go charging through. But if what you are reading is a poem, then I think you don't need that interference, if you can figure out a way to get around it, to do without it. And that was the other great discovery for me here, that this started with punctuation, and as it compressed, and as I played with it, I suddenly realized I didn't need commas and periods and dashes and so forth.

The other thing, the other great discovery, after twenty or twenty-five years of writing poems in a particular way, by and large: not all my poems, but most of my poems have been composed in terms of a specific process. Images would sort of juxtapose, or ideas, or found objects, whatever, would juxtapose for me; they'd set up a juxtaposition. Suddenly they'd ring because I had come in contact with them around the same time, by sight, by hearing, by reading, whatever. And I would sort of carry those around in my head as they bounced and started setting up relationships. And eventually, sometimes that day, sometimes two months later, I would sit down to write that poem. I had done considerable editing in my head by then, literally playing with it in my head, so when I sat down to write it, I had a pretty good idea— not of what I was going to write—but of what was in there to use. So the poem would come out, usually quite quickly. I'd read it over and go right back to the typewriter and do a second version, which usually consisted of doing two things: cutting out extraneous sections, things that in that first shot had come pouring out and seemed not to belong; and cleaning up the areas where the syntax seemed to be getting in the way of the poem, where I again, writing fast, had written stuff that just didn't work once I read it. And that would be done immediately after the first draft, and then I would sort of let the poem sit overnight, and the next day, or at the most, two days later, do a third version which again, was not usually serious revision, but tightening, to make it behave the way I wanted it to, usually not adding something, usually taking out things that now appeared to be extraneous, or tightening syntactical setups. Now what happened with this poem, and has continued since, is that there is an extensive series—I don't remember how many revisions I did on this, but in terms of revising, now—I know on *Houses* and on *Cacti* there were as many as thirteen or fifteen drafts. And a lot of those drafts, consisted literally of games-playing within the line breaks, within the syntax, just trying every possible variation, trying to get it to sit right, to read right. So that there was, first of all, much heavier revision. Now second of all, what came with that, especially with the longer poems, was that for the first time in my life I discovered that I could write over a period of time, that I didn't need to get it down all on one shot; I started *Cacti*, I wrote a couple of pages, and then either I had to do something or I just didn't want to write anymore, but I knew I could continue it, and that had never happened before. Even the long poems before that, stuff like *The Fourth Ark Royal*, which you haven't seen because that's in *Just Friends* . . . but longer poems, like some of the ones in *On Occasion*, had been written—you know if it was going to be long, then it just had to be a long siege at the typewriter because there was no way to stop half-way through and pick it up again. I had to get that whole thing down. Now, I found that I could do this.

Now, what I mean by playing—because that's important to me, and I think especially to those of you who do want to write poems like the ones we write these days, where line breaks, it seems to me, are critical—most of us start by depending on our ear. I mean if we become poets, or think we're going to become poets, certainly one of the things we possess is an ear. You know, it "sounds right," it "feels right." I think you have to get used to the possibilities and really write them down, not just read them out loud to yourself. In *Cacti* and *Houses* there were three-line strophes with maybe seven words in them where I typed every possible permutation and combination of line breaks and run-ons. Start considering the kind of grammatical substitutions and play with them, or transpositions, or vocabulary changes. It's that kind of playing that I'm talking about—just allowing yourself to touch this thing. I mean look, I know full well how we all feel about our tender green leaf. We produced this poem and it's there, and it suddenly becomes something magical, and we're terrified that if we touch it, it's going to disappear. And I don't expect you to start out doing it because, God knows, it took me twenty-five years to get there. What I'm suggesting is that if a poem seems to you not to be working, play with it that way; take a deep breath and let yourself start changing words, lines, line breaks, always keeping your first shot so you have that initial inspiration, and you know what it's like, you know where it came from. And not only write them down, but read them aloud to yourself. It ain't only in the head, as you all know.

CLASS: Something happened in *The Woman Poems* to make that happen. I expect that's for someone else to say, not you. You've got to keep the scholars busy, but have you really tried to work that out?

J.O.: What do you mean, "something happened"?

CLASS: Oh, something that would produce this change. Maybe there's no connection, maybe it would have happened anyway, but . . .

J.O.: Well, by the time this "new" poem was written, after the marriage was over and my life had changed, I was now a single father, taking care of two small children, and I was once again a Village stud out prowling. Three years earlier, I might not have even seen there was a woman sitting in the park, so there were certainly a lot of changes that had taken place in me, but I'm sure you're right too, in the sense that I talked of a few minutes ago, about *The Woman Poems* being the last shout of the old line, the old way to write poems for me, and I moved on to something new. That was the way, what had to be said had to be said then, and then having done that, you work and you work and you work. You finally perfect the triple somersault, and after you've done that on the circuit for a couple of years, the audience may still be excited about seeing it, but you've decided you want to try something else. And I think that happens inside. I mean I'm not talking about a commercial decision. I'm saying if what you are doing is really of interest to you, then you don't want to keep doing it the way you learned how to do it. And then there is also the adjustment to new conditions. Look at the way Carl Yastrzemski bats now, compared to how he batted when he was twenty-four. Maybe I can't hit the fast ball anymore out of the old stands. In a curious way, of course, a lot of what I'm doing now is closer related, in sheer form, to the poems I did in the first two books, in *The Dutiful Son* and *The Love Bit*, the kind of attention to line that's going on now. But that's again more technical than anything else. It's interesting, I suppose, to someone who is desperate for something to write about in some Masters course, but I don't think it's particularly interesting to anyone else.

CLASS: Maybe, but I'm looking at the "Poem for the New Year, December 31, 1973" in *Names, dates, & places*. I assume that preceded *The Woman Poems* and the long poems.
J.O.: Yeah.
CLASS: The "old poet" comes in, and you told me that was . . .
J.O.: Olson.
CLASS: It happend in a dream, and Olson came:

> i am saved
> by the old poet, he helps me
> break loose. he tells me
> he's never yet seen one would
> hold on if you fought long enough

and later it's:

> he said: hold on, hold on,
> until the new vision comes.
> it comes, it opens up,
> it always comes.

Now I'm maybe just trying to be too precious, but you have opened up to something like an invasion.

J.O.: I'm seeing things differently. It will be hard for you guys to believe this, but that mid-life crisis happens. You get to be thirty-eight, forty, forty-two, and unless you've already died, and a lot of people have, either by choice or necessity, suddenly you find yourself, literally, in Hell. You have no idea why you're doing what you're doing, why you're where you are; you can't see any value in anything you've done before, and any value conceivable coming up ahead; and somehow you have to make that journey down to Hell, that Orpheus trip down to Hell and back up again, and come out with something. From another aspect, Pound quotes Brancusi, I think, as saying that every sculpture he'd ever made was the product of an idea he had when he was eighteen. Now Brancusi made that statement when he was in his mid-thirties and already established as a great sculptor. What occurred to me later, having gone through this and then thinking about other people—poets, painters, sculptors, etc.—who had gone through the same trip, that one of the purposes of that trip is that you've run out of, or gotten bored by, those ideas you had when you were eighteen. You've finally written them out, and now you have to find new material, and new ways to look, new ways to see. And I'm not talking about novelty for novelty's sake. It's literally that you are bored sick with what you know how to do. And you're tired of it. And so, if you come out of it, if you face up to that hell, if you let yourself die and come back, you come back with new materials, new ways to look, and naturally, your voice changes.

Your voice contains within it the seeds of what went before, but you're looking in a new way, and you're seeing new things.

So that now it's possible to make leaps like *Cacti*, which is a poem I could never have written in the twenty years before it, or a poem like *Houses*. I mean my life is changed in the same way. Teaching, which I shunned for the first twenty years of my adult life, suddenly became not only available, because lots of things become available and you say "No thank you," but seemed intriguing, and it turned out indeed to be interesting and intriguing. I started writing for a newspaper when I was forty, and again that was the kind of writing that I had said "I've got to avoid because it will steal from the poems." That's why I worked in a print shop, because that let me be close to words, literally, but didn't put me to what I considered a draining drudgery of cranking out words. Now, suddenly, I was forty, and I found that I could do that kind of writing and not only didn't it bother me, but it was fun, it let me say something, and it became its own thing. So you go through those changes, and you do come out different. That's the prime thing that happened, I think. I hate to make it that simple, and it ain't simple. When you all get there, I hope you will all think of this moment and say, "Jesus, the old son-of-a-bitch was right." And I hope you will also remember that it's possible to get through it. There's a very famous poet who, as far as I can tell, just got terrified at finding himself in Hell, and fled, went back up, refused to fight it. And the result is, that if you look at the work that he did—he died, I guess, at sixty-five or seventy—if you look at the work he did for the last twenty-five or thirty years of his life, it is an absolute repetition, badly done, of the great stuff he did before forty. And that's e.e. cummings with those wonderful, magical poems that just flooded out from him for twenty years. Suddenly, you look at the last books, and they're just pale imitations, and dumb and boring.

CLASS: What I wrote in high school is totally different from what I'm writing now, but I had to walk around for two years with all these things in my head that I didn't want to write down, because, when I first started writing, I wrote a lot of images because I thought that was how you were supposed to write. And then for a long time I walked around with ideas about myself, direct statements about myself, and I was afraid to write them down because I thought, "Gee, you're not supposed to talk about yourself; you know, who wants to read stuff about yourself?" But now, for some reason, I'm writing about myself, and I'm getting used to it.

J.O.: Yeah, and you will keep going though changes, and you'll keep discovering new material. You know, for now, clearly, it's right for you to be writing about yourself, and you've been able to accept the fact. Ten years from now, or five years from now, or a year from now, or twenty years from now, you'll say, "I don't want to write about myself, I want to write about the big world outside," or whatever. You learn to trust those changes. I mean I get bugged sometimes—I hate to say this in this class which obviously loves both *Cacti* and *Houses*, but sometimes I read *Cacti*, and I really get furious at what I take to be a self-indulgence in it. And yet I know it's a good poem. I know that it says not only something that's important to me, but that, happily, turns out to be important to a lot of other people, that revelation that comes at the end, that kind of self-knowledge. And yet, there are times, reading it, that I say, "Jesus, Joel. Can't you lay off? Is there nothing in the world but you? Is there really nothing in the world but dumb you?" So, that doubt is always there, and the impulse is always there, and you've just got to learn to ride with them both.

CLASS: In that thing about e.e. cummings, maybe the reason he didn't want to change was because he had a sure thing.

J.O.: That's part of what happens too, sure. Sure. But part of it can be simple fear. You know, what the British call "funk." Which I never really understood, but the word always meant it for me, literally. When they say, "he funked it," it really is just hiding your head and fleeing.

CLASS: Don't you think that part of the inspiration or motivation for this kind of change that you're talking about is the result of the fact that everything around you is changing, and it calls for new tactics, poetic tactics, that the people who are listening to you want you to speak in another voice? For example, you were mentioning that your work became more sparing. Do you feel that it's a valid statement to suggest that in recent years there has really been a trend toward the tightening of language? We're not so flowery and so verbose. The whole picture is tightening down, perhaps as a result of taking a look at Japanese poems and these real, tight little image poems.

J.O.: It may be, but my own feeling is—certainly most people who talk to me about my poems, and certainly most people anywhere near my own age, invariably talk about what a wonderful book *On Occasion* is, which is the last book before *The Woman Poems*; they tell me that they cried themselves to sleep with it the night before, or they were re-reading it, and it's the most moving thing they've ever read—I think the reverse is true, that people get used to a voice from you and get a little bugged when you change that voice. Now if I were starting writing, what you're saying might be true, that today maybe people expect the sparer thing. But I think once you've established some kind of voice that people have come to expect, and then you go through a change, they get upset. They say, "Why are you writing like this? The other stuff was so gorgeous." And, in fact, you then have to say, "The other stuff bored the shit out of me." There are poems in *On Occasion* which are good poems, and which say things to people, but when I was writing them, that one level of brain that keeps looking at you and telling you what you're doing kept saying, "Oh, here you go, you're writing a Joel Oppenheimer poem." And I knew that I could write a Joel Oppenheimer poem. I knew that David could call me and say, "Hey,

I'm starting a magazine, send me a poem tomorrow," and I could sit down and write a Joel Oppenheimer poem.
[After a break on the tape, the discussion has returned to finding oneself in Hell.]

CLASS: He sort of ran out of Hell; some people just stay there

J.O.: And some people go and can't handle it and stop. They go down there, and they try, but they can't make it.

CLASS: Maybe it's biological, and some people are tougher, but maybe also in that new vision that's in that poem there are things that come, that if you didn't fortunately have them available . . . —and Charles is one of them too. And I don't mean to suggest that he was literally somehow leading people, your Vergil, taking you right back up

J.O.: Well, why not? You need help, you know; the best thing you can do is confess that you need help.

I have to throw two statements at you, because they are very useful. The first is from Delacroix, the French painter:

> If you are a poet when you are twenty, it's because
> you are twenty.
> If you are a poet when you are forty, it's because
> you are a poet.

This is isn't as arrogant as it sounds. All it means is that at twenty it's easy to do a lot of different things. And first of all, all of us are, hopefully, immensely spread out at twenty. You're playing the trumpet one minute, and making a sculpture the next, and writing a poem the next, and playing baseball the next, and dancing your ass off the next, and getting boxed and talking all the night the next. That's what happens. The energy is there, and you haven't quite decided what it is you want to do or you can do, and in fact, you're trying a lot of things, simply to find out if you *can* do them, or even if you like doing them. But to stay with something, and to keep growing at it, is a different proposition. That's what this is saying, that to still be writing at forty, to still be painting, to still be doing whatever it was you started with, with the same energy, care, dedication, means that you've put yourself through a change, and now you're focused, and now—like I go out twice a year and play in the annual Lion's Head "Over-forty, Under-forty" softball game, but every pitch I throw reminds me of what has happened to my body. Or once in a while, I go out and dance all night, and remember again what has happened to my body. Or I sit with people, and I have nothing to say. I know it's hard for you to believe, but, hey, I've got nothing to say. And the only thing that stays constant is that I still write poems, that I still am trying to figure out how to say what I have to say. So that's what this means.

The other one I got from Gerry Gilbert, one of the Canadian "sound" poets who's been visiting, and I don't know where he got it; I think it's from the Chinese. It's wonderful:

> He who reads 100 poems writes like 100 poets;
> He who reads 1000 poems writes like himself.

I've never been worried when either myself or other people, friends or students, suddenly seem to be imitating someone. I worry if it goes on, and if it never moves. I had one student a long time ago, Michael G. Stephens, who has published a wonderful novel called *Season at Coole*—which is barely available, but if you see it, it's a wonderful book— and a couple of books of poems. And when I knew Michael, when he worked with me, he was about twenty-one, twenty-two. He would come in—we were working a workshop together—and he'd come in with a batch of poems, and I'd read them and I'd say, "Oh, you've discovered the Cantos," and he'd say, "Yes," and for three weeks I'd get nothing but fake Cantos. And then all of a sudden, he'd come in and I'd say, "Oh, you've started reading cummings," and he'd say "Yes," and for three weeks I'd get cummings. He did it quicker than anyone I ever knew. I mean, in a year-and-a-half, he ran through every major voice in English and American contemporary poetry. He did it, learned from them, got out quick, and went on to the next. Very shortly, he was writing his own poems. So this is very useful. If you read a hundred poems, you are going to write like a hundred poets. But that's great. It gives you a sense of how far you can stretch yourself and what the possibilities are. And then eventually you will find, if you keep looking for it, you'll find your own voice.

CLASS: I think one of the fine things about writing poetry is that the muscles that it takes to write poetry don't deteriorate the way the ones that it takes to play baseball do; therefore, it can be a life-long thing.

J.O.: And in fact, the truly great poets, with very rare exceptions, are the ones where the work gets increasingly stronger. For me, of course, simply because he means so much to me, the classic example is William Carlos Williams, whose early poems delight me and whose middle poems delight me; but his last poems, particularly the ones written after his near-fatal stroke, when he was in his seventies, and clearly, literally, had been threatened with death, they just knock me flat on my ass. This man, after a lifetime of writing, just got stronger and stronger and stronger. Muriel Rukeyser, who died too young —I think she was about sixty-two when she died last year— for years, for me, had been sort of an interesting poet, but not someone I would go out of my way to read. She appeared in all the proper anthologies, and I sort of glanced at the poems and moved on to somebody else. They were there, they were competent, etc. The last ten or fifteen years of her life, they just came on stronger and stronger and tougher and tougher and harder and harder, in both what she was talking about, and how she was talking about it; they were just incredible. And I don't think that really happens in many other areas, that you get better as you get older, if—if you put up with those continual descents into Hell. If you keep learning, if you keep yourself open. And as Alice just said, you have to keep doing it, but at least you know that if you keep doing it, it ain't gonna be like baseball, where no matter how you keep doing it—the day is going to come, no matter what he does, when Pete Rose can't hit, because his body just will say, "enough." Some of you may not be too young to remember one of the most awful things I've ever seen, which was Willie Mays in the 1973 World Series, at the age of 42 or so, going back for a line drive that was not an easy catch, but the kind of thing that for twenty years, well, and if you count his childhood days, for thirty years, he had never had a bit of a problem with. And all of a sudden, it was an old man, who looked like me, literally, stumbling and nearly falling down, while the ball sailed over his head and bounced against the wall. And I nearly cried because here was one of the most magnificent athletes I'd ever seen in my life, and ever expect to see, and he looked like me, you know, he looked like me. And that doesn't need to happen in poetry. It can get better and better. It gets different. I don't want to take away Williams's early poems because they were marvels of their own, but, Jesus, what happened at the end was unbelievable:

> I cannot say
>   that I have gone to hell
>   for your love
> but often
>   found myself there
>   in your pursuit.

A wonderful line to be able to say to your old lady at 72. Or,

>   It is difficult
> to get the news from poems
>   yet men die miserably every day
>   for lack
> of what is found there.

[Joel then reads *Cacti*.]

    Now, one way you know that you've done it is if you read it three years after it's written, and you still get cold prickles up and down your spine. Now that doesn't necessarily mean that that has to happen for you guys. All I mean is, it happened for me then, and you know, that little voice I talked about was saying, "Holy shit, Joel, you really did write it."

Now, there is one other point about that change process that I should mention, which is that things happen in that poem that I had never allowed myself to do before. There is a certain kind of personal assertion there, like the end of the second section, about the crown of thorns and me facing each other with our hard beauty, etc. I could never have allowed myself to talk that way about myself before. Now, at this advanced age, I can say, "Hey, fuck it, like I'm here. I survived. A lot of people I knew have died already, or have stopped doing what they were doing, and I'm here." I can say that stuff. I can make a *statement*. And if people think it's ego, then too bad, but I've gotten here, and I know what it cost; and I'm allowed once in a while—as long as I don't beat people over the head with it—I'm allowed to make a statement of fact. If you look through the entire body of work before, with a lot of poems written about me in it, I never made statements like I make in this poem. And it was a great feeling of release, like, "Oh, wow! I can say that!" And that was an important point. The main reason I, at least, and I hope many of my brethren stay with—keep writing poems—is that, in the end it is fun, it is exciting, it is fulfilling. Don't snicker if it ain't happened to you, because if you're lucky it may: writing a poem, and knowing that you've said what you want to say the way you wanted to say it, getting those prickles up and down your back, is the closest thing I know to that feeling the Spanish call "the little death," that wonderful feeling immediately after a beautiful sexual experience, that total draining, and at the same time, total fulfillment. It's the only thing I have in my life that compares to that. They both happen just about as seldom. Oh, I'm not complaining. That they happen at all is the wonderful thing.

The Woman Poems

J.O.: I had read the Bly article, the essay, "I Came Out of the Mother Naked." Six months after that, at a summer conference at Thomas Jefferson College in Michigan, a whole bunch of us, including Creeley and Bly, Phil Whalen and so on—there were about twenty of us there—had been together for two weeks. I had talked a little to Bly about the essay, and he had delivered a couple of what were supposed to be seminars but, in fact, turned out to be lectures by him about The Mother. I had been really terribly moved by the essay, but not in terms of using it in any way; it was just something I had read that I thought was terribly important and moving and wonderful. Then a few months after that—now wait a minute, that conference was in the summer of '71, and I must have talked with Robert first and then read the essay later that year. And then a year after reading it, the spring of '73, these poems started bubbling out. The first three poems,—"The Lover," of course, was a very early poem from *The Dutiful Son*—"Every Time Wondering," "Gettin' There," and "The Lady of Madness" were all written six months to a year or a year-and-a-half before the main text. But from "Moving Out" on it just came pouring out in a real frenzy. I felt for the first time in years that the Muse had come in and was sitting there; that sounds romantic, but it was a really strong feeling; I mean these poems wrote themselves to a great extent. The first six were written in about a day-and-a-half, and the rest just kept bubbling out at a slower pace, but still the same bubbling. And I was aware from the beginning of "Moving Out" that, obviously, I was dealing with material that had first been loosed by the essay. And it was as if it had sat in me for a year, a year-and-a-half, tying in with my own needs and perceptions, and it was there to be used when I started writing. In the meantime, I had also, obviously, to some extent, digested it for myself.

The kind of vision I have of the Mothers, I think, is different from Bly's. A year-and-a-half after the book came out, Robert Bertholf, in despair, bought me a copy of *The Great Mother* by Jung's disciple, Erich Neumann, because he felt that having written the book, I really ought to read what Neumann had to say about Her. I tried—I like to try to help my scholarly friends by reading the books they think I ought to read—and I got about a third of the way through, and I noticed that there were many significant differences between both what he gave as the classical readings of the Mothers, and the Jungian readings, and my own. But at the time I was writing the poems, obviously what had happened was that Bly had triggered a great deal in me. I responded to it immediately and went off and used it. So yeah, certainly there's a debt there. And I toyed for awhile with the idea of even saying something to Bly in the beginning of the book, but then that seemed kind of hincty. It just didn't seem to make much sense given the direction the book had gone in. Perhaps I should have—well, I guess if there had been a preface . . . —but I just wanted to get into it really. And I was saying to David last night that what happened with the "prefatory" poems was simply that as I was writing these new ones, about halfway through, it occurred to me—these three poems began nibbling at me, that I had written in the year, year-and-a-half earlier—and it seemed to me that they were, in the classic sense, prefatory. I had been reaching for the material and hadn't realized it. And so I put them in, in effect, as preface. And what I had wanted to do, and what just never ended up being done, because I didn't have that much control over the book itself, was to set them aside as a preface, literally, a page here saying "preface" and a page here saying "The Woman Poems." I guess two more pages would have broken Bobbs-Merrill, or something, so it didn't happen. I don't know that that would have clarified anything particularly, but it would have been more the way it really happened.

CLASS: We had all discussed the book and we were all fumbling with the Mother myth, knowing little bits here and there and trying to share what we did know, but then when the article was brought in, it just kind of all clicked, and possibly the way it did for you, only, like you said, it loosened up the material for you. And for myself, possibly speaking for the rest of the class, it brought things together nicely. Some of your poems we just couldn't at all get any kind of direction for, or squeeze in, or discuss, but that article helped me to understand them.

J.O.: Well, there is no doubt in my mind, just from the fact we chose the two forms we did, that Robert was speaking specifically to an audience. I mean, an essay is, in effect, a written-down lecture. The poems, while I obviously hope that they talk to other people, are, in one sense, as I've said before, an answer to a question I've asked myself. If that answer is meaningful enough, and if I do a good enough job of writing it down, then it works for other people too. But a poem, it seems to me, can't be meant to act the same way an essay does. It can end up "teaching," but that's not what you sit down to do; whereas Robert clearly sat down to say, "Okay, this is what I know, and this is what I think, and this is what I want you to pay attention to." That's a different process. And I'm glad it came in that way, in this case, that the essay was available to you, because I think that makes absolute good sense as a help in clarification *after* exposure to the poems.

CLASS: Okay, as long as we're clarifying things, perhaps we had better bring up one of the other questions we had to ask you: what about some of the words that you use in your poetry?

J.O.: Like "Mother"?

CLASS: I can read them, and still not be comfortable with them, and we just want to know how you can use those words.

J.O.: Well, first of all, I suspect that there are places in there where I don't intend you to be comfortable with them, where I want them to work that way. But this is a question that has many different aspects. Some literary history, first of all. One of the things that a lot of poets in my generation felt it was necessary to do—I don't know if it says how old I am here, but I was born in 1930 and I started writing poetry essentially, say, 1950—one of the things a lot of us found it necessary to do was to break the stranglehold that the then all-powerful world of academic poetry had; the Eliotics were in full force, and where they weren't in full force, there were merely remnants of the old Victorian ideals. Both groups, really, were primarily interested in keeping poetry an elitist art available only to a small percentage of specifically educated people. They were terrified of all us beasts out there, and had been; they'd been terrified of people like Pound and Williams. They had to sort of accept Pound a little bit because of his erudition, but they didn't like what he did with poems. They certainly weren't going to pay any attention to Williams, that primitivist doctor, or to people like Oppen of Reznikoff or Zukofsky, or to people like Olson, a guy like Olson who was using his erudition the wrong way. Certainly one of the things we did, encouraged by the general loosening of morals that took place during World War II, when the boys got off the farm and saw all those places in Europe, was to assault the language, literally, to start ripping down a lot of that stuff, to say, hey—"fuck" is really a cleaner word than "intercourse" or "cohabitation" or "coitus" or "fornication," or all those words that, somehow, you could use if you had to. And certainly better than a euphemism like "making love." If I had written these now, I suspect I might not have used them that much, but given where I was, both in my own head and the age I was at, and what this book represented in terms of my poetry, I had to. At the time I thought it was a breakthrough book, but I realize now that it was the last energizing shout of what I had been doing all along, and that the poems that came after constitute the changeover. And so in it I went back to a lot of those things that I had believed in very strongly, a need for cleansing the language. And that's what we were doing, really. We were saying, "Hey, listen to Confucius and call things by their proper names; don't cloud up the issue."

On a poetic level, rather than literary history, the kind of stuff I was talking about seemed to me to call for that language. I couldn't talk about this material in pretty words or roundabout words. As I said, some of the times it was necessary to shout at myself, and to make me uncomfortable, to make you uncomfortable. There are some poems in it I have a terrible time reading aloud. There are some poems in it that I've never read aloud, other than to very close friends. It's the material as much as the words, of course.

There was also, and there always will be, it seems to me, a need to—not force your culture to listen—but to try and break through to some people. This book was also written at the height of the sort of separatist frenzy, in New York City anyhow, between men and women. It was a time when there were an awful lot of women deciding to abolish any contact with men forever, you know, when the readings started that said, "No men allowed no matter what you think; you just can't come in." And I think probably, knowing my own whacked-up head, a lot of me was saying, "Goddammit, some of you are going to be able to listen past the words." And it was important because, obviously, one of the women in the poem—not the only woman, but one of the women in the poem—was my then current wife; the marriage was breaking up and had been, was breaking up for a lot of reasons, some reasons I did understand, and a lot that I didn't, and a lot that had to do with what seemed to me her buying wholesale a lot that was in the air. And certainly some of the poems respond to that, or talk about my response to it. But that's part of it too. I don't know if that connection is so obvious. It was a time when Adrienne Rich would write a letter to the *New York Times Book Review* and, in an out-of-context paragraph, start screaming that Charles Olson had had no right to write a line that read, "the curve of a woman's breast." A male poet was not allowed to use those words. So some of the use of language is a response to that, to that kind of assault, to say, "Hey, I'm here, and these things exist, and if I have to scream it, then I will." Now that, of course, wasn't conscious. I'm talking after the fact. But I'm sure that that was part of what was working in the poem. What I was saying, and what I'm happy to say happened over and over again, and I hope happened here with some people, was that that very discomfort that caused shock or anger forced people to read deeper into the poem and to see, in fact, what was happening in the poem, which is something I think ought to happen. You don't need to do it by using four-letter words; it's a process that ought to happen more often with poems, and I think does happen with poems that move people. Something in it grabs them, but something at the same time is disturbing them. It's the fight to move past that, to break through, to get some sort of epiphany about the poem, that allows the reader to supply the same kind of energy that hopefully the poet supplied to it, and that makes us love poems, makes us end up saying, "Wow! That poem changed my life," or "that poem taught me something," or "that poem solved a problem," or "that poem really made me happy." I think it's that process, that the poem not only gets to you somehow but also holds you off somehow, and you try and resolve that. And in this case, I think, what was doing that, to a large extent, was the language on the surface, and that there was enough happening otherwise that was pulling you toward it. It made some people sit down and really read it, or really listen. A distressing thing that happened right after I'd finished *The Woman Poems* was that when *On Occasion* came out, which collected poems I'd done earlier, people kept walking up to me and saying, "I loved your new book." And I kept thinking, "How did they know? How did they know about *The Woman Poems*?" And then I realized that they were talking about *On Occasion*, and I got terribly depressed. *On Occasion* is a bunch of nice poems, and I like a lot of them in there, and I'm not at all disavowing the book—I'm not saying, "Gee, I shouldn't have published it"—but I'm saying in terms of what the poems in *On Occasion* are doing, and what this is doing, there is no question in my mind that this is a book full of a much different energy and it will live much longer than most of the poems in *On Occasion*. And while I know that the poems in *On Occasion* are more accessible, far more accessible, it's because they're dealing with the surface. In the end, who cares? Sure, they're lovely, and you could type them and hang them on the wall, or you could send them to your mother, or your lover, or your child, and have them learn something from them, I suppose; or you could read them to each other at a party and everybody would be delighted; but they are not saying, they are not attempting to deal with the universe in any way near the way poems like this are. I mean, that's my own feeling about it. But one hates to pick between one's children. So that's like saying, "I like this kid much better than I like the other ones." They are all great kids.

CLASS: Would possibly the strong language, instead of making people grab hold of the poem, stop them?

J.O.: I'm fully aware of that. But at some point you say, "Oh the hell with that, this is what I have to say." By and large, when you are writing a poem, you can't afford to worry about reaching everybody. We know that anyhow. And certainly, when dealing with material like this, you reach a point where you're making decisions on the basis of how much it will change the poem. And if it will change it too much, you just say, all right, I know I'm throwing away part of my audience. But again, I have to say, there have been enough incidents—classic one: invited to read two years ago, three years ago, at a small college in North Carolina, in the eastern plains, the coastal plains. That has nothing to do with Black Mountain. It's in a solid Bible-Belt town. The college itself is not only basically a college set up for backwoods fundamentalists, but it is dependent to a great extent, for its funding, on the older fundamentalists in the town. Literally, that's where its money came from. And I was all set to read anything except *The Woman Poems*. I'm not a fool. I may be lots of other things, but I'm not a fool. Or like the guy said, "I may be crazy, but I'm not stupid." To my horror, my host spent fifteen minutes in the introduction delivering a paper which talked to the point that *The Woman Poems* was the most important book published in America in ten years; how there were many things in it that would upset many people, but that it was a book that had to be paid attention to, and that it spoke to many of the key problems of our day in terms of relationships between men and women; and he went on and on. And half of me was saying, "Gee, isn't that terrific! Sombody really read the book." And the other half of me was saying, "Oh fuck. Like here is this audience, and the doors are all down at the other end of the hall. There's nowhere to run." And I got up and I said, "Listen I'd like to read some of my other stuff first, and then I'll read a couple of *The Woman Poems*." I read some of the other poems. I felt like the response was okay. And then I took a deep breath, and I had to, I mean he had put me under the gun. He had done it with all the best intentions. He believed, and still believes, that the book is terribly important. And I'm delighted. I'm delighted that there is someone teaching in a college like that who thinks that what I'm doing is good poetry. That's wonderful. It seems to me it would have been impossible twenty years ago. It was hard enough to find anybody in a school like this who knew what a poem was, no less a five-hundred, six-hundred-student religious school in the depths of North Carolina. So I took a deep breath and I read, and the response was absolutely incredible. Elders of the church, and middle-aged matrons, after the reading, both to me and in the following couple of weeks, in speaking to the host, and in letters to the English department, talked about how their first impulse had been to just get up and leave the room, but they sat and they listened, and they were glad they listened, and they were delighted that they had been forced to pay attention, and that the poems in fact had spoken to them, and on and on like that. It was an incredible experience. And I've been back there since, and I get a really warm welcome.

The dean of the college is a guy whose whole academic training was in small religious schools in the South, a genuine Southern Baptist, with all the strengths and all the weaknesses. Up here we tend to stereotype it, but you know, there are strengths and weaknesses in backwoods Southern Baptists. And, by God, the second time I went, he called me—I was in another town in North Carolina—he called me specifically to ask me if I would give an informal reading at his house, to just a small company. He wanted to invite some friends from the faculty and some friends from the town and a couple of students, but to feel relaxed about it, to do it in a living room setting, rather than a formal reading. There was that kind of response all through. Now I have to feel that something that I never would have attempted on my own, that I got forced into by somebody else's love for the work, turned out beautifully, that an audience that really would never have read any of my poems, not only listened to, but learned to love the toughest of them. It was fantastic. So I have to believe that what I had hoped was happening in them, is to some extent happening.

In the middle of this, I begin to feel a little weird, like it's turning into a whole ego-trip thing, and I don't want that to happen, if you can excuse that end of it, because obviously there is a pleasure when a book of yours, a thorny book, is responded to in circumstances like that. But hopefully, we can avoid the ego end and just talk about the poems.

CLASS: I had a question about the mythology. You said before that there was a pretty big difference between Neumann's writing . . .

J.O.: Yeah, well, I'm not much of an expert on his, but in his various drawings of the representations, and his talk about it, it looks like our cosmogony is a little bit different.

CLASS: You were talking about a difference between your handling of the myth and Bly's, and the Jungian readings, but there seem to be three different kinds of readings of the same material. I'm not too familiar with Olson and the way he looks at mythology, but it seems to me that in some of his later writings he talks a lot about mythology as being kind of a representation of an image of the world that is there for the poet to manipulate. And I was just curious if you were familiar with Olson's handling of the myth, or if that had any kind of effect on how you deal with it, because obviously you're taking material that's kind of general, if you take the idea of the archetypes as being from a kind of collective unconsciousness, but obviously you're using it really personally, so I was just kind of curious if Olson fits in there or if you have any thoughts on it.

J.O.: Well, it fits in there generally. But not specifically. I haven't read that later material. And yet, I learned from him this sense of the myth, that the myth is real, that the myth is a realer view of the universe than anything we have, and that, in fact, is what we use in our poems and in our lives. So, having had something triggered in Bly's essay, I immediately swallowed it whole and allowed it to work in me, and came out with what amounts to, certainly, my own playing with the basic myth, but one that I can make sense of, and I think I can defend, if I have to. What I was talking about was that in the Neumann book there are various circular charts representing either the tripartite mother or the four-part mother.

[Joel writes on the board this diagram:]

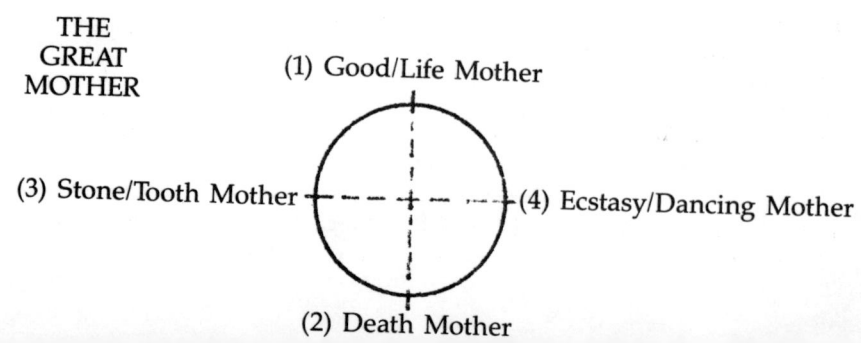

There will be various images and representations, like the following goddesses constitute this area, the following constitute . . . and so on. And I was sort of astonished because I had been working in the blind. I had been literally working off my own reactions to the initial trigger, and I had come up with a rather, to me, complete grouping. And I was just a little astonished and puzzled by the fact that my grouping was different from Neumann's, and was different from Bly's. And yet I knew mine was right for me. That's the Ankh: Good Mother or Life Mother is up here, and Death Mother is here. And this axis is like physical or real, to use offensive words; and this is like Stone or Tooth Mother, and this is Dancing or Ecstasy Mother, and this axis is spiritual or imagination or whatever. What I talk about for instance, in "Moving Out," is a life-long fight along this axis (3 to 4), with the fears of either being hung up here and unable to move either way, or being sucked into Tooth Mother and turned to stone, with the yearning for Dancing and Ecstasy Mother and a total acceptance of this. Now that's me. There are other writers—well, the one that came immediately to mind was, strangely enough, William Saroyan, because he wrote a long essay, a long preface to one of his books of stories, and all he talked about in it was how all writers in the world either are running towards death, or are fighting it off. And of course, he put himself in the group that was fighting it off. And I had read that a long time ago, and I didn't believe him. I understood what he was saying, and I knew he was saying it was true for him, but I didn't believe the "all writers." And when I came to this, I realized, of course, literally, this axis doesn't bother me at all (1 to 2). I'm alive now; some day I'll be dead. I'm not going to say I'm going to be a hero when I'm dying. But what I'm saying is that in my life it doesn't worry me, that I was nothing before I was born and I'll be nothing after I die. And I know a lot of people that does bother. What bothers me is this: I'm constantly being torn between these two mothers (3 & 4). And Saroyan was saying—he just got too general—that everybody's hung up on this (1 & 2). No, half the people are hung up, or I can conceive that there are people that are hung up this way or this way, and they accept the others.

CLASS: I was going to say, your mothers in the book seem to float between each other; they seem to blend more than any kind of separation.

J.O.: That's because Great Mother is Great Mother. What the concept involves is that, sure, we can talk about this (1-2) or this (3-4), but what we're really talking about is this (the whole circle). And that was the whole point of it, and that's what Bly talks about in the essay, that what we've done, he says, in America, in the twentieth century, is try to cut her out (3), to say that she doesn't exist. Remember, he talks about that, that rejection, that denial of Stone Mother, and the fact that in our myths the only Stone Mother who remains alive is Medusa; whereas, originally, every time there was a form of Ecstasy Mother there was a form of Tooth Mother. Every time there was a Death Mother there was a Life one, and so on. And now we've tried to live with just these three (1,2, & 4). And we've said that's too horrible (3). And what they had sense enough before to say was, "Hey, here's Great Mother and she's got all these manifestations. She's all of them. And they're all equally frightening and equally attractive." And there are people—we know it—who are terrified of Life Mother, of Good Mother, of Earth Mother. I know my mother, my own personal mother, was this lady here (3). And I had a friend who had this mama (1), and God, I envied him. And then I got to be twenty-one, and I said, "Wait a minute, that must have been ghastly." Like George used to tell me these stories at seventeen that sounded so terrific, about how he'd come home from a date (my mother would be waiting up, but the door would just close in the bedroom as I entered the house, but no communication). George's mother would come in and chat with him. Like, what went on? was she a nice girl? what did you do? And he had all these terrific conversations. And when I was twenty, I said, "Jesus, I was lucky. Like what a terrible way to live." And they're all, all around us, and they're in our lives, men or women. It is one whole Mother, with different manifestations.

CLASS: Did you just have a book published called "Fathers" or "Fathering"?

J.O.: I'm writing it now.

CLASS: Oh. Well, where do the fathers fit into the mothers?

J.O.: Those are different fathers. The fathering I'm writing about in the book is Reality Father. I mean, I'm a single father now. It occurred to me I've been a father most of my adult life. I have a lot of kids by different relationships. And I've had about every kind of relationship to my kids that it's possible for a father to have. I've been a standard nineteen-fifties father—bring home the money while she runs the house; I've been a visiting divorced father; I've been an absentee father; I've been a raised-consciousness father in a relationship; I've been a single father. I've covered the field. So what I'm talking about there is: what is it being a father? And certainly, underneath it I suppose would be the mythology.

I draw certain conclusions in here. I really never went into that, but obviously I was concerned with how men meet the Mother as opposed to how women meet the Mother. One day I did sit down to ask, who are all these mythic men, father figures? And the tie-up there is that Good Mother is with the Spring King, the young king who gets killed every year and is the young virility figure, the young husband figure, the one who makes the queen fertile, and then gets killed. Death Mother is with the thunder god, Yahweh, Odin, whoever, the one who controls life and death, or controls death, anyhow. Stone Mother I've thought was with the sea god; we are creatures who can't live in the sea. And Ecstasy Mother I made the classic tie-up with Dis, Pluto, the god of the underworld. Like where the magics are. There's a marvelous, terribly male chauvinist poem by D.H. Lawrence from the twenties. The point of the poem is that Persephone doesn't bring us Spring; Dis gives us Spring because when Persephone sits there bitching because she's been doomed to the underworld and insists that she has to go visit Mama, Ceres, and when she runs away, Dis sends the flowers snapping at her heels, to bring her back. It's a classic Lawrence poem and I love it, and I've loved it for twenty years. Of course, that's where Ecstasy Mother finds her mate. It's not a satisfactory mating because how can Ecstasy Mother ever settle for just Dis? But that's the only one she can have any real solid connection to, is the god of the underworld, where the mysteries are, where the magics are. So now I'm not prepared to make an Ankh out of these four, but what I was trying to do was to reach into my own myths and say, all right, who makes sense—that's a funny word to use in terms of myth—who makes sense as the partners for these manifestations of the mother? So let's see if these four make it.

CLASS: Did you feel like when you were all done that you had reconciled it somehow, that you'd been able to get the Great Mother embraced?

J.O.: Yeah. And I also felt some of each of the gods in me. As in any of us. I could feel: oh yeah, once upon a time it was this. Once upon a time, a lot of times it's been this. Rarely it's been this, and rarely it's been this. [Points at each of the mothers.] But it has been.

CLASS: But it's not going to be number three anymore.

J.O.: God, I hope not. I hope not. I mean that was my relationship with my mother; it was my relationship with one of my wives. And I hope I've had enough of that.

CLASS: It's almost like what the mythology says, you have to learn to include her because to ignore her is to be destroyed.

J.O.: Right. But that you don't need to live with her. You're allowed to say, "I know you're there, and I did what I could, honey, but like leave me alone; I don't want to be here." So again, in the most serious sense, this is playing. Playing in that primal sense of letting yourself and the world around you create some order instead of trying to impose it on it. Saying, let's see what happens if.

I don't want this to be thought of as Bly's essay. If I were anywhere near that stage of thinking about it I'd sit down and write an essay, or instead of sitting here like this, I'd be delivering a pre-formed little lecture about it. I'm still playing with it. Mother still comes into the poems. Not as directly or as heavily as here, but it has become a natural thing for me to use in some of the new ones. You know, every once in awhile she's there because she belongs there. In a way, I feel like I've been born again, like I got back to Mama and now she's part of my life. For a lot of reasons, I hadn't realized she was there before.

CLASS: You said last night that you thought now you were doing the real writing, and that it was the tough writing. Does that include these?

J.O.: Well, this is the hinge.

CLASS: And now, so much of what you're writing is the long poem.

J.O.: It's gotten a lot longer.

CLASS: Is that the natural result?

J.O.: I have to assume part of it is a natural development. The first long poem I wrote is in that book that Jonathan's bringing out eighteen years late, and there were a lot of problems about it. Gil Sorrentino hated it, said it wasn't a poem. LeRoi Jones looked at it and said, "I don't know what's going on here." And Charles came to town—he was staying at LeRoi's—and we all went out one night, and after we came back, I said, "Listen, Charles, I know you're on vacation, but I've got to show you this poem; can I come over tomorrow?" And he said, "Yeah, sure". I dropped it off, went out and had a beer, and came back. Charles met me with a big smile, and he said, "Well, you finally did it." And I said, "What?" And he said, "I've been waiting for you to start writing discursive poems, because clearly, that's what the voice was crying for, like you were cramped in those little poems." It took me a long time to believe him, and a long time to learn how to do it, but I think now that's what that line really is, precisely. It's discursive in the best sense. But also, aside from my own search for my own voice, I suspect that if you write long enough, and pay attention to what you're writing, I mean if you're not just repeating what you wrote before, or not committed because you think you have a position to uphold or something, to writing a certain way, I think you do, naturally, start stretching more and more. By and large, most poets—not all poets—but most poets, do have more to say when they get to be forty-eight than they had when they were twenty-eight. And when I'm sixty-eight, I'll probably be writing endlessly. Part of it is that things do come more together. I hate to admit that, since my life is going in seventeen directions. But in fact, because you narrow your life to some extent, you cut out a lot of the bullshit, or at least you avoid it as best you can. Things do pull together more, and they become more unified, and it's more possible to write a longer poem. When I was young, I saw things in isolated little things that made isolated little poems. And now I tend to see things in long connected strings. And like I say, I think part of that is just a natural development, and part of it is specific, because of where I'm at, where my voice is at, and what I'm looking for. But poetics isn't my strong point. It's hard for me to theorize about this stuff. I can make guesses, and I tend to trust the guesses, but I've never sat down and tried to write it formally as a theory.

Do you want me to read a couple of poems?

[Joel reads "Gettin' There."]

J.O.: Somebody say something. I mean this is the first time I've had a chance to read these to people who have spent some time with the book. So rather than me reading to you, I'd rather you say, "Hey, read me a poem."

CLASS: "Prayer Poem II."

[Joel reads "Prayer Poem II."]

J.O.: Now that image that keeps reappearing in here of the contradictory sides of Mother, the clearest image of that—those of you who have looked at the Neumann book know it—are the Indian statues of the mother: one hand is beckoning, and the other is holding off; one hand is armed; it's the six-armed guard of the goddess; all the arms are doing different and contradictory things, and it's all there.

[Joel reads "The Lady of Madness" and "Mirror Poem."]

CLASS: Could you go back to page 57,

>   if
> it was only my
> wife alone i would
> not worry, would
> consider it fashion

and talk about before when you spoke of this whole separatist fashion that was happening in New York City at the time that you wrote this, and saw your wife getting caught up in it, getting caught up in the fashion, if you will, of this thought. Here, it seems to be a little bit different. You said, "if it were just my wife I wouldn't worry." It's very direct, your relationship with your wife and your relationship to what's going on. I could hear you saying if it were just everybody else I wouldn't worry, but it's you, buying this wholesale and I am worrying.

J.O.: No, what I meant was that if, in fact, my wife had started wearing this kind of blouse, inside I'd be saying, "Oh, it's terrific, like she found this terrific thing to wear." But instead, everywhere I turned, all these women had them on, and then, that's where the jump to the myth was. Oh, they are mirrors, they are holding me off. Even though they're lovely blouses, and they're lovely women and they've "handsome rounded shoulders," (I love that line) the image then became Stone Mother. It wasn't an individual decision by my wife to wear it, or that terrific woman that we saw at that party; it's that everybody was wearing it, and there was a purpose to it, there was a meaning to it.

[Joel reads, by request, "Discovery Poem."]

J.O.: Anybody know who "Li Po" is? Chinese poet from the seventh century A.D. A man with whom I feel a great deal of connection. He was a terrific lush. He was a particular favorite of the Emperor. He enjoyed a high post and much wealth and many favors. And one day he committed the unforgivable sin: he put the make on the Emperor's favorite concubine, and since he was a marvelous poet, and a wonderful man, she accepted. He then committed the second unforgivable sin: he showed up three hours late, boxed out of his skull, and he fell asleep on her bosom without consummating the act. In a fit of pique, like they used to say, she blew the gaff on him to the Emperor the next day. He was immediately banished from the court and sent into permanent exile, except that he was a wealthy man, and the Emperor genuinely liked him, and, in fact, the Emperor sort of admired his balls. He had really tried to do it. And if he hadn't liked drinking more, he would have pulled it off. So the exile was being sent to small mountain town, which, to someone used to the high court life, was a drag, but it wasn't as if he was living in a hovel. He had servants, and he had a home, and he had his poems to write, and he had the wine shop in the village, and he wrote many, many letters to old friends, and he wrote a lot of good poems. Just—it has nothing to do with this, but it's part of the whole thing—he did write the finest lush poem I've ever read in my life. It's a poem about waking up on one of those early days in Spring, when you know Spring is coming. And he sits out on the porch in the morning, and he has breakfast, and he looks, and it's wonderful, and he thinks about coming alive, and he starts sipping a little. And somewhere in the middle of the afternoon, he crashes. When he comes to, the day is done, the moon is coming up, and he's blown it. This is the first perfect day of the year, and he has blown it. And he's furious with himself. He's so furious that he cracks open another bottle. And the last line of the poem is, "two hours later I was dancing with the moon." Now, he died, they tell us, coming home from the wine shop one night. The village, as I understand it, was at the headwaters of the Yellow River, up in the mountains, and he had written millions of poems to the moon. He was coming home, and there was the full moon reflected in the river. And he looked at it, and he said "The time has come. I've written you all these love poems, and here you are and it's time for us to make it." And he took off his clothes and wrote a little poem, left it all under a rock, and dove into the Yellow River to fuck the moon. And he was never seen again—I mean they found his body, but he was never seen again. And I always thought that was kind of a glorious way for a poet to go.

He's a guy I feel close to. And this poem is about that sense of it, that service to the lady. There she is, and we've been writing her all these poems. Hey really, it's like you meet somebody at a party, and you're both really cooking, and it's terrific, you're really talking, and suddenly it occurs to both of you that you don't really want to talk, you want to go to bed. And you don't know how to handle that because you've been thinking all along that really you're not interested in that, with someone this terrific; we're supposed to be higher than all that. So that's what that poem is about.

CLASS: That's what I meant in class about taking this very literally. A lot of times even the myth of all this becomes secondary to the real relationship of it all. That makes a lot more sense to me.

J.O.: I think most myths are literal, really, if you look at them. That's what they're about. They're about life.

CLASS: Not as literal as the situation you just talked about.

J.O.: Oh, I don't know. We've gotten the myths watered down a lot, but read the early versions. I was shocked when I discovered that I had been lied to about Aphrodite. Aphrodite comes from Kronos' sperm hitting the ocean when they chop it off, when the gods do in Daddy, and they castrate him. And as they castrate him, some sperm shoots out and hits the ocean, and Aphrodite appears. We're not told that. But the Greeks knew. And the people they stole the myth from knew it even better I'm sure. I mean we're so far from it.

I read a book this summer that really turned my head around. It's called *America B.C.*, by Barry Fell, who's at Harvard. If I say too much about it, it will turn into a two hour session, but he posits, with rather strong evidence—and with none of the fake scientific stuff about visitors from outer space—he posits on very sound archeological and linguistic grounds, settlement of the Americas by Europeans as early as 1600 B.C.. There's a lot of fantastic material in it. One of the things he raises as a speculation and that I bought immediately—it's just a little side thought on his part—but he's talking about the phallic monuments that are found among many of the Celtic peoples and that are found here, although they haven't been recognized as Celtic, for a lot of reasons he goes into. Connected with them are a lot of little ceremonial altars, with little bowls in them, with runoffs. Whenever they see one of those in Maya land or in Aztec land, they say, "Aha, blood sacrifice. Bring on the virgins and let's go." Fell makes a very strong case for it being, literally, a puberty rite of young men, being forced to prove that they can come, a ritual orgasm for the goddess so that people know that they're men now, that they can, in fact, take a wife and have a child. Again, it's easier for our culture to say, "Blood. Those terrible, awful people. They were cutting each other up." The thought that maybe there was a ritual where a kid got up and jerked off for the goddess is horrifying. Everybody runs home screaming. It can't be handled. So it's in that sense that I think myths are a lot more literal than we think, that they tie to the things we know about and that we worry about. That's what myths were made to handle, the things we worry about. I think little kids worry about blood. I know what Lem does—seven years old—when he gets a scrape, and there's a hint of red about it. There's absolute terror. But I also know that sheer terror I felt at eleven-and-a-half, twelve years old when Joey Swick told me—because he was thirteen—what happened when you came; the absolute awe and terror and fear that this could happen, the worry about it. And myths come out of those things.

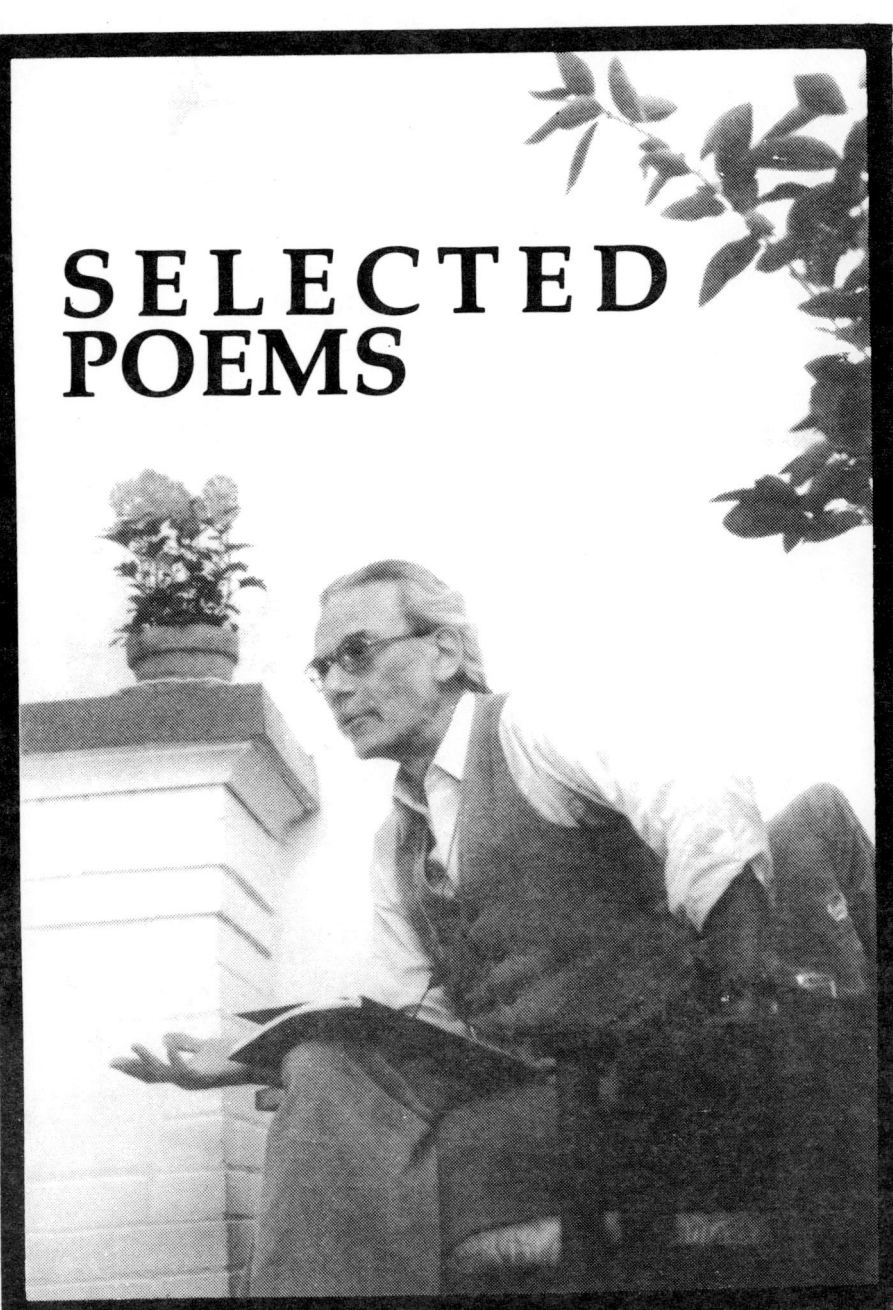
SELECTED POEMS

from **THE DUTIFUL SON**

THE BATH

he will insist on
reading things into her simplest act.
her bath, which she takes
because he wills it so. her bath
she takes to cleanse herself.
ritual. ritual always
in his life. she takes her bath
to ready herself.
and himself more often than not decides
she wants him unbathed. manlike.
what he is most pleased about is
her continuing bathing.
in his tub. in his water. wife.

THE LOVER

every time
the same way
wondering when
this when that.
if you were a
plum tree. if you
were a peach
tree.

from **THE LOVE BIT**

A FLOWERING AVOCADO TREE

i am reminded
of the flower
which opens bit
by bit, along its
scalloped petals.

a seed moves, a
seed germinates

by parable, and
brute force of
image we have come
to your hopeless
avocado seed.

        it has lain three
        weeks in the jar
        you prepared for it,
        resting on crossed
        toothpicks, enough
        of it submerged that
        it gets its juice.

        even your avocado seed
        has hope. it may still open!

christ, say it again, even
a hopeless avocado seed
may still open! it/s
the simplest of songs!

and burst from its
inmost places a
blossom on a stem, leaves,
and all the green
ichors it needs to survive

within it.

MID-PASSAGE

as if i were going to make
myself over, or, starting
from scratch, cultivate
me, i got some new
glasses, a haircut, allowed
the barber to trim up my beard.

soon, i/ll have a new cap, and
maybe a derby, i/ll buy me new
slacks, shoes, two or three pairs.
i/ll do myself up, and the
poem will emerge fresh, shining
as a tulip on easter morning, my
friends will invite me to dinner
my wife/ll curl langorously in
bed. like a tulip easter morning.

MARE NOSTRUM

a bosom of
green buds,
ass like a
valentine.

the spring
rolls around,
moiling me
up.

(also green buds on
hedges, my heart
in every dogwood
blossom, even tulip,
even pink daisies)

i'm forced to it again.
                      old
lady with a
bosom of green buds, also
an ass like a valentine, etc.

AN UNDEFINED TENDERNESS

an undefined tenderness came
into the relationship. we were
afraid of such things, still, it
became necessary, and we learned
not to put it down—or put it
this way, time and a senseless
friction wore a smooth edge.
finally, i think, we could face to it:
there is no love possible beyond
those first moments of fire and
trembling passion. this makes more
sense than a roomful of roses,
your ass, my heart. and, desire
burns fiercely in me yet, i
ought to be satisfied.

from **IN TIME**

A NOTE

in the touch—if
not there, not
at all. head and
heart open and
close in their own
concerns, skin only
does not lie or
delude itself. the
hand reaches out
while the mind
considers, the
hand grasps while
the soul adds it
up. the hand
rejects or accepts
while all the rest
play games.
              it/s only
a game the rest says
while the hand, furious,
is furiously involved.

ZOO STORY

olaf the
walrus at the a-
quarium—remember that
the adult walrus can
take on polar
bears—was for so
long swimming there with
seals only, when they
finally came up with
a lady-love-to-be, and
put her in (tho she
was not yet of age, quite).
it took hours before
he knew her for
walrus even. then he
clutched onto her, and
held for five hours.
the keeper, then, fearing
for her strength, had
her taken out.

walt you sing of
yourself

THE INNOCENT BREASTS

the innocence of her
breasts. the way in
the soft morning, as
she leaned over him,
reaching to see the
time, they hung tender
and innocent.
                    just
six hours earlier, as
in many other beds,
they had been hard
and passionate as
pomegranates, and a
few hours before
that, every man at
the party wanted them.
go further back: ten

months ago they had
been filled with
milk, and the boy
suckled, and the
man held back his
hands and lips—now
they were not his.

we are all, we know
now, bone-pickers after
darwin, rag-pickers after
marx, brain-pickers
after freud—we are
trying to reconstruct
our history. breasts
are a sexual attribute.
the chimpanzee's flat
chest with long nipple
is more efficient for
feeding. the breast is
a sexual attribute. they
hang warm and innocent
in the morning.   four
hours later, at the
forum, fortunately or
not, those breasts took
over the conversation.
after all man is a
political animal also,
and can figure a way
to breasts even with
war. but she was embarrassed,
saying, they/re not
even that good. and he:
you didn/t think it/d
mention your ass, did you?
and the politics of
breasts leads men into
madness, tumbling over
each other in a
mad race for a
sight, touch, taste.
i won/t be blamed
for it—i unabashedly
stare through every
see-through blouse,
look down every low

neckline, peer carefully
through the right
kind of armhole. it
is nobody/s fault, we
are born to love them,
even though they are
difficult to make
love to.
      the buttocks
at least are truly
functional, allowing
man mobility, agility,
speed. the breasts hang
innocent in the morning
light. at night they
tighten in desire; in
the evening they peep
provocatively. the
young man asked plaintively
whether lenin had ever
wondered about the cup-sizes
of fellow revolutionaries.
i hope so—this is how
the revolution gets
made.

      in the morning light
he ached to touch them,
catch the weight and the
softness in his hand, but
could not. some obscure
idea made him just watch,
while she thought him
still asleep. they were
too innocent in the
morning light. he thought
it no time for the carnal,
though he laughed as he
thought that. he preferred
the thoughts he was
having, to the action—
not perversely, but as
a special delight.
      besides,
after the forum, they
would nap, in the warm
afternoon, and the meat
of it, the true carnality,
would carry them. the
breasts hung innocent
in the morning light

OLD STORY

a man was out walking his
totem one day and
got lost
      *but the
map is not the
territory* he kept
screaming. neither
was the territory. and
tho he invented fire and
bent his opposable thumbs and
laughed and constructed
memory, he sat there alone with
this big goddamned bear next
him.

    when the woman found
her way to that neighborhood
she was in all her trappings,
her nine breasts bare, the
three little titties (32A),
the three big boobs (38D), and
the three leathery dugs (unknown),
and on one side of her
back the spinning wheel her
uncle had made her, and on
her left arm the leather
gauntlet for the bow over her
shoulder. tho some of her
arms were reaching out
others were pushing away, but
she had never seen fire
before, so she sat down.
it was also unclear to her
as to which was the bear.
soon this was discovered and
she turned into a reasonable
34 or 36, b or c cup. he
took one of her arrows, chopped
it in half, added a six-foot
long straight piece of locust
in the middle, and found himself
comforted able to stand up
holding this while she
slept. the bear kept growling
much of the time, as if to
say: hey bo, let/s get
out of here.
           one day she

came upon agriculture.
the bear kept growling,
and every day the man laughed
with the bear, tousled its
hide, and turned back to
her. she still had all
those different arms, but
he thought there was a
key to that too, as to
the breasts. when the
crop of grain started coming
in he said to her: i
think i/ll sit down and
invent whiskey. the bear
kept growling.
              next, for
want of anything better to
do, they made a house.
he said, later, it was
to keep the bear out. he
figured he could stand
or sleep in the doorway,
holding the long arrow.

some say that that
first night in the house,
all her arms except two
disappeared, tho those
two kept all the
designs of the others.

in any event, she
said, now you/re dealing
with reality. when
you invent whiskey, this
time, or peyotl, for i
forget which end of the
territory we/re at, it/ll
be religion, and good for you.

he put down the long
arrow and took her
to bed, where they lay
happily for a while, in
all conceivable positions.
then he invented writing.

from **ON OCCASION**

FOR DAVID

eyes wide, we
have dumped it
in your lap. you
do not know that
yet. hands open
and closed, the
panorama stretches
before you. you
do not know that
yet. lips ready,
you will take all
we have to give you.
and will survive.
and will pay us
back in our own
coin. even love,
if we come to deserve it.

FOR WILLIAM CARLOS WILLIAMS

i am angry because
there are still
birthdays
        and yet they
tell me you
are bad off . that
you are dying
        that
the last time you
went off they
thought you
were gone
        (at the
same time they
say you are
furiously
jealous—

                    that someone
else can still
use a
right hand!

they tell me you
are an old man

they say when
you write new
verse they will not
take the
last one until
you write
the next
          they are
afraid you
will decide it
is all you
have to say.

it is
difficult to
talk about

: how much land
you moved
into
     it is an old
story
no one is much
interested
          especially
in the face of it
that you are
still at
it.

the inheritance
will not be written
down and cannot be
contested

which is why there
is a need to
say something to
you . said straight

out without the
dignity of
image even—
             since if
you are dying then
you do not need
images now . rather
we should save
things to put
next to you which
you loved and
needed

that it should be
a good trip
           that you should
still be able to
move as it
was

(old man i
am living on
that land, developing
it, i.e., raising
houses and
cutting the timber

—like a dutiful
son the father
hates

—and it
makes me ashamed
sitting here
           no
matter how
busily

FOR MATTHEW, DEAD

8 august 1967

at four, it seems to me, he
fell off the stump by the
mess hall, bruising the
hell out of his forehead
and nose, and a good deal
of screaming went on.

how shall we scream now,
when at twenty, he slipped
on a wet, moss-covered
ledge of north percy peak
and fell one hundred yards to
his death. at least this
made that decision for him:
he will neither serve in
lyndon's army, nor go to
jail, nor go to canada.
he was trying to scale the
peak by the west trail.

one half hour ago my own
son at eight months fell,
tripping in his walker over
a raised lip of door.
it will not appear on the
book page of the *times*,
and we laughed instead of
screaming, to soothe him
down. this one has almost
eighteen years to make
his choice, and every day
a peril. good christ,
there are easier ways to
have decisions made. twenty
is no good time to die.

MORATORIUM

wednesday, 15 october 1969

the little boy wasn't three yet,
and as the crowd grew, carrying
candles, it was hard to know what
he thought about it. he, himself,
wasn't carrying a candle but had
a large corrugated cardboard whale,
it had giant teeth, and he held it
high and proud. four people looked
at it and said noah the whale, and
one oohed moby dick, but most didn't
say a thing. it was a silent march.
the little boy got tired, but he would
keep walking, so he gave the whale to
his father. now it rode high above
the crowd; people were asking what
is it? and, why carry a whale in
a peace march?
                     i tried to answer
that they were dying more quickly than
us, so it seemed to make sense. some
looked at the two of us very strangely,
a few heard what we were saying.
                                       they
are killing the whales so fast that
the fleets come back half-full ahead
of time—and a male blue whale can
swim his whole life without ever
finding a mate. this should tell us
what sort of a beast we are, how we've
learned to draw leviathan forth from
the sea, and kill him. from the
beginning we knew how to kill ourselves.

FOR JOHN AND LUCY

21 november 1970

aha! spring's a
long way off. the
bears shuffling into
caves. the world
slowing down, the
days gray. one
last fling 'til
sun comes back,
one more time
touching, feeling,
the wedding bells
will ring.
         the
bears find their
way slowly, they
do not choose quickly,
they spend the
year opting for
this berry, this
particular salmon.
ah, but when the
choice is made!
oh, most true of
all the zoo we are,
the bears.
         the caves
we sleep in are
the burnished thrones,
our ladies bedazzle
the universe.
         and
we nose our way
slowly, feeling the
year as few do,
picking the snow or
the spring or the
run of the fish or
the perfection
of the honey straight
out of air. go, let

the dance begin again,
let the cave glow
while the bear and
his lady sing, and
the world turns,
as we do, slowly,
and the spring
begins to build again,
endlessly. it will
greet you to wake
you soon, and
the world will
bless you, with
all its good things.
amen.

THE ONLY ANARCHIST GENERAL

the architecture fell into
place only at night, the paths
led somewhere, the lights
lit them, even the low
wall had a reason finally,
it comforted me walking.
my wife questioned my
orders as if i wasn't a
general. the bridge still
frightens me, *not* the ravine,
which is why it is necessary
to make friends with trolls,
constantly. still, i met my people
halfway home, and walked back in company.

my wife questions my orders as if i
were not the only self-taught happy
genius of my household. i note
crests and rises, point out
defensible positions. the
armies move and swell, the
battle is coming. my wife
questions my orders. i am an
anarchist general shouting orders in a
strictly formed landscape. my children
did leave me here knocking on wood,
i walk the bridge alone in the night's
landscape, thinking of low
walls, covering the terrain.

ZEN YOU

as we were involved in this
dart game where nobody seemed
able to hit the bull's eye, which
was necessary to end it, i
turned to my partner and said if
i use zen, that is to say, if i
worry only about the dart and
allow the dart the problem of
the target, perhaps?

                    good
christ no! he shouted—worry about
the fucking bull's-eye and let the
dart take care of itself, for
christ's sake.

              i took aim, carefully.
the dart flew straight to the bull's-eye.
oh well, this is the west, we
do things differently, i suppose.

from **THE WOMAN POEMS**

GETTIN' THERE

twenty years ago i
knew about love. now
i am tired. i study
primary needs.
i wonder about cowboys
going to sleep on
stony ground, their
saddles their pillows,
the hard day behind them.

they twist and stretch
finding the curves they
will fit to, they fall
to sleep gently because
they are tired. the
way i am tired it is hard
to go to sleep, because
i have not been working,
i have been fighting.

gunfighters also go to
sleep hard, because they
are not cowboys. i was
referring to the working
stiff, the man earning
his bread. i was not
referring to the quick
dazzle of sunlight on
polished barrel, the
challenge, the long
drawn out stare, the
tension. goddamnit i
was not referring
to shots fired in
streets in front of
saloons, or tables
turned over.
          like any

old gunfighter i
dream of the ranch,
working together,
going to sleep in
a bed as rocky as
the ground because that
is where we have learned
to sleep. but tired. i
dream of being tired
enough to sleep gently
and deep and not dream
hard enough to remember.

what terrible visions does
she have in her sleep,
my dale evans, who used
to work that bar in
dazzling sequins, and
also slept uneasily, and
is tired of it.

            we dream of
the sunset as the time to
lie down, we dream of banked
fires to be raked
in the morning not
night. we dream of
such hard labors without
tension that the
days of tension without
hard labors will
someday fade into the
sunset. then i
will know about love.

PRAYER POEM II

mother gives and
mother takes away.
mother comes close
mother goes far.
mother suckles and
weans mother
does all things
each in its time.

give me strength.

mother give me
strength or take it.
i do what i can
in your service.
is it fair to mark
me for this? there
is no fairness she
says only life. so
the service is
ended. to begin.
again. again. again.
the service begins
again. give me strength.

THE LADY OF MADNESS

i did not know what
madness truly was until
i heard the truth. she
spoke without lying calling
things by true names.
it was madness.
she said, you were the
ugliest thing i had
ever seen—i was
fascinated.

        i understood
that word as with a
snake. i had never
dreamed another would
say this. i thought it was
my thought, and
lovers, therapists had all
disabused me of my own
notion. i thought i
was beautiful.

        she sat
in my living room and
with her crazy honesty
told me the truth. the
ugliest man she ever saw.
she was fascinated.
i listened fascinated
by her madness and
watched her body freeze
and thaw. she was mad.

MIRROR POEM

women i love and
watch these days walking
around mirrors bits of
glass in their sleeves,
their shoulders, set
glinting in light and
sunlight, in dark
corners of bars, medusa
i think of, the
stone mother only
approached through the
safety of mirrors to
look on her with
open eye straight you
turned to stone, stone
mother did this, stone
mother i know, why
are these women wearing
mirrors bits of
glass in their
sleeves set on their
handsome rounded
shoulders, to keep
my eye glancing
off? to distract
me? to lure me
on? that is
unlikely. they
are mirrors, mirrors
keep you from real
objects, objects are
real but not in
mirrors, your
hand slides over
the surface, quicksilver
was what they used
to make mirrors
from in alchemy.

as if in a stone
set polished in your
belly or your
tooth i was to see
the world, when i

ought to be looking
direct. your belly
button straight into
where you live. no
stone. no mirror.

is this the totem
of their being?
mirrors? stones?
i tremble as i
walk, as i look in
dark corners of
the bar, light
corners of the house.

how came this
mother to my life?
how came medusa? i
tremble as i walk and
look. it was her
sister. it was
her sister. i wanted
her sister. i thought
her sister was here
beside me. i will
fall, turned to
stone, and cannot
move. the mirrors
are my signal who
she is, always. if
it was only my
wife alone i would
not worry, would
consider it fashion.

it is so many women
i look at these days,
mirrors flash and
blind me, stop
me cold as stone.

DISCOVERY POEM

lady, sister, lover, mother,
woman, i have called and
called my whole life for
your presence, asking only
that you visit. i have promised
faithfullness, i have written
as you tell me. they are only
words. when will you
live with me, be more or
less than inspiration? i
want to know those most
secret parts of you, and
let the poems go damn.
i want to fuck you as
li po tried and died.
i take my chances. would
you have it any other way?
you answer only prayers,
and this is proper. i
can give no more prayers,
and this is proper. i
want to fuck you, and
if poems still come
then that will be alright,
but that is secondary.
i have discovered what
is secondary, what is first.

from **NAMES/DATES/PLACES**

A LETTER TO PHILIP

can i any longer address you dear phil
when i have spent the morning
ordering my life in unrealities

the rent the food the clothing
the ten percent allowed for luxuries
the baseball register and the sporting news

which things are necessary in my world i say

i have written my oldest son
and sent a check to celebrate his nineteenth year
and i have yelled at my youngest son
to celebrate his curiosity which stalled my writing checks

my head is awhirl with money and games and family
and you are in the real world finally

now you are not only my brother
but the world's brother and the ant's brother
god's brother and even the foolish writer's brother

which is why i wonder how i dare start a letter dear phil
wanting to know the honorific when you must recognize none such
but there is a need to honor you somehow
as you honor me by every step you take

i think of you sitting silent sitting speaking walking
and i am honored
                    i have been given this grace to know a decent man
who does right things while i whirl in unrealities
writing checks and poems

E.P. 1885-1972

for a long while you
were owned by everyone,
an object, an
enemy, someone to
defend or excoriate;
owned but not sold
you said come my
songs we will sing
of perfections we
will get ourselves
hated; you said every
day as the sun rises
make it new; you even
said a long time ago
we elect either knaves
or eunuchs to lead us;
you were talking of
america; you were
not a nice man; you
taught us all the
language and you
reinvented the forms;
you lived these last
years in silence, telling
us something more; you
walked naked all your
life putting your
life on the line for
the taking, you were
bought, owned, now
you are dead and in
the perfect way of
this world, now
only the poets can
own you, barter
your brilliance in
their lonely rooms,
parlay your winnings,
fight over your
coat you never once
turned, now the
world is done with
you and only
the poets own you.

SERVING NOTICE

i will not be
that single daddy
my friend had
roasting a leg of lamb
every sunday
slicing neat slices
through the week

these kids
will eat differently
every night

their clothes will fit
and not be put up with

and they will wear
their hats and rubbers

and in my bed
i'll dream whatever dreams
are necessary

and i'll curl those bodies
i can or want to
around my body

and i'll take the necessary time

and i will not make
leg of lamb each sunday
slicing slices through the week

CELEBRATING THE PEACE

9-15 may 1975

if you celebrate the end
of a war you are celebrating
that war.
        go home my
townspeople into your own houses
that is where peace begins.
                      the war is starting
what speeches will you make
or hear that have not been
made or heard by you before?
                      the war is starting again
in what way by gathering
to reconstruct air that was before?
how by gamboling before the orators
on sunny days to make a peace?
                      the war never ended
you are gloating you are waving
flags in triumph.
                no god no master
the flags said in paterson so
long ago the silk strike the
only flag i wish to see no
wars no governments no states
they take umbrage like a human being.
                      the war goes on forever
forget the dead people, forget
limbs piled in earlier bloody
wars, forget blasted innards, eyes
seared, leaves gone, earth scorched—
yes we did that too—forget
homeless people, peopleless houses,
forget helicopters falling in the water,
forget the gold that weighs those choppers down.
                      the war is over but a ship has been
                      captured by them and retaken by us
                      and the choppers have landed the marine
no rhetoric will make it as it was.
the nature of peace changes by the war before.
dead grandparents would not recognize this peace.
and theirs would not recognize the peace they knew.
so many wars.
              there is no peace
if you must celebrate it. parade parade
march your banners and your selves you

are victors you have triumphed over
other people you have won. what? you
have won what? peace is the absence
of a triumph it is quiet singing in
your house and bed it is turning to
your own concerns and pleasures.
                      there is heavy small arms opposition
                      the enemy has released their captives
stop celebrating. *celeber*: frequented
or populous. wars. occasions of wars.
they are frequented, populous, the
people stream one way or the other
under orders or because of fear. peace
comes from *pactum,* a bargain, a bargain
made that we shall be left alone.
                      several choppers were downed in the assault
                      the ship has been returned
                      the men are safe
                      the marines are still engaged
let us lay down this burden down by
the riverside, let us feel peace
in our hearts and minds let us have
no more celebrations that celebrate
what we have beaten lest we forget
what it was was won and we become
conquerors and strut as certainly
as jack boots in another place.
                      the fighting goes on
                      the war goes on
crow triumph. peace cannot ever win.
destroy the word to save it. we
have heard that before.
                      there is no peace
build such a chain of people
you will not need to celebrate
you will not need these gatherings
except for the work of hands. these
other works will destroy us every time.
do not go to the party. do not
celebrate the end of war you
celebrate the war
                      there is never any peace
                      there will never be peace
                      the war goes on
                      the marines are landing
                      we don't take shit from anyone
                      we'll show them
                      peace is not a victory but a natural state
                      do not celebrate the end of war

from UNCOLLECTED POEMS

ACTS

my son and i
walk out
in this cold october morning
toward his school

we hold hands

his other hand
holds a pennywhistle

he will use it
to accompany the guitar
in the morning singing circle

at each corner we cross
i am looking for you
while he and i walk and talk

i keep thinking
we will meet
at one of those corners
our paths intersecting
just as the clear note
of the pennywhistle
occasionally crosses
a particular chord
of the guitar
in the structure of some song

i keep thinking
in other words
that there must be a point
that we cross in common

and so this morning
we do meet
and walk together
half a block

he and i still
holding hands
you next to me
on the other side

one small moment
for you and me
to register our selves

and then later
after he is in school
and you are gone
i drink my morning coffee
and read the paper
again intersecting
this time with the world

i read that hugo zacchini
the first human cannonball
is dead

i read that all his life
he wanted to be a painter
and that after his retirement
he taught art to young kids

'yes, say for me'
he is quoted
'that my cannon
does me much honor
but do not
forget to add
that it is as a painter
that it is my ambition
to be known—
day by day
my cannon cannot give me
the thrills
that i can get
with my brush.'

lucky man who
day by day
first in malta
then throughout europe
then in the old garden

before me
a little boy
holding my father's hand

went one hundred and fifty feet
reaching an arc of seventy-five

where was my father headed
what intersection
was i going toward then

a flash
a puff of smoke
a roar
and he would go
hurtling through the air
in an idea
he conceived
serving with the artillery
in world war one

so i hurtle toward you
and toward this poem
aiming for some corner
of our lives
where we can meet
this morning

i do not know
whether or not
there is a net
it never occurs to me
to wonder about it

the flash smoke and roar
take the forms of
an alarm clock
and the radio
and a small child
needing his bottom wiped

oh this act also
will be carried on
by my son
just as his son
learned to enter
the mouth of the cannon

oh i also wanted
to do something else

oh i also learned my methods
in some previous wars

HOUSES

eighteen years ago
i left your house

it was your house

yes i brought home
the money
         we
did it that way
in those days

now again
i am showering
in your house
         "her bath, which she takes
         because he wills it so . . .
         in his tub. in his water. wife."
         was even more years ago

         i do remember
         and i don't

getting undressed
i saw a silk robe
hanging behind the door

and the jars of oils
the soaps and powders
lining the shelves
beside the door

all in neat order
beautiful things

things beautiful
by themselves
and things beautiful

i thought how all
that i have loved
all that i have missed
is in this house

don't misunderstand me
i am not speaking
of romance
or rekindled love
or even second chances

nor is it a new obsession
with neatness
from one who's always
been the other way

if anything it might be
a lesson for lovers

perhaps even
for the ones
i come here
to see married

our first son
and his beloved

as if that action
by our child
allows you
to invite me
and me to accept
and that is why
i am in this house
far from my own

far from that house
i have learned
my own lessons
building

in any event
a lesson
here also

> in first love there are things
> we grow to as a habit

                and will never be happy
                without again

                                sexual appetites
                change
                        it is easy
                to grow cramped and leave

                still i say again
                no matter what reason
                for the ending
                                there are things
                we grow to as a habit
                without which
                we will not be happy

so it is
that years ago
i learned to love
your ways
so clean and neat

ways that cared
for beauty
and were beauty
and were
without
compulsion
          they happened
around me
without my knowing
and they were
caring ways

i've smiled at times
these eighteen yeaars
realizing that
the only reason
i have folded up
my washcloth
in my bathroom
is because
you wanted it that way
instead of crumpled
                while
all that is remembered
of our sex

are bits and pieces
of some short-lived scenes

no touches
no movements
underneath me

a few sighs
or groans
a few importunings
one to the other

a picture of your breast
or thigh or face or hand

but i remember
very well
the house
you gave me
and see it
here again

perhaps this is why
i am so pleased
that i have changed
to see it
through the eighteen years
for what it is
and what it was
for me
    not that
you have not changed
it's clear you have
it's clear we both have
but this part of you
has not
    and the part of me
that sees it has

* * * * *

now it is after the shower
and i have changed
in a much simpler sense

i am in some
new found finery

a fop or dude
inside my western shirt
my shiny boots
and all the rest
as you have never seen me
and i feel i fit
in your house now
a stranger perhaps
because i am so proper
where as your lover
i stuck out
        it is
the proper way to visit
i am saying

but on your shelf
among the oils
and powders
is the frog
i bought you
our first christmas
twenty-five or more
years ago

i see it now

made of brass
a candleholder
on his back

        i knew
you wanted it
i saved the five
or seven dollars
that it cost
      i'm glad
to see it now
        it means
you really wanted it
it wasn't just a fancy

you kept it with you
and you use it now

there is a stub
of candle in it

perhaps some nights

you bathe yourself
by candlelight
                i
see you that way

long baths as
i remember
            while
i lay in bed
reading
        or wrote
that first book

the one with poems
about you bathing

or just waited
in our bed for you

the waiting was not
always good
            it
destroyed the marriage
i have sometimes
thought
        but not
the waiting
while you bathed

that was part
of what you gave me
as i lay in bed
and dreamed
            a sense
of preparation and
of love and care

it was the other waiting
caused perhaps by what
i did to you or
what you thought i did

then after a while
i could no longer
and i went
            you were just as happy

and that pain
is gone now

i remember only
there was a woman
of rare beauty
                a wife
who bathed herself
so slowly in my tub
that i wrote poems
about it
        in that first home
i ever had
        a home you gave
to me long years ago

* * * * * *

before the shower
i had taken a nap
in the guest room
of your house
                  i
dreamed of us
of course

we were naked
but only from our waists
on down
        as if to say
this is where we are
right now
        with the sex
outside and open

we were so afraid
in those days
and we didn't know it

in the dream
our tops were covered
our brains under cover
covered prettily
to face the world
and each other

perhaps that
might have worked
if we had known it then
to cover up our brains
and let our sex hang out

but we didn't know it
and we kept on talking

so i woke from that nap
this afternoon in your house
at peace with the dream
despite its sexual content
which aroused me
              it was
not you so much as
talking to myself
the good doctors
tell us that

at peace i went into
the bathroom for my shower
where i found my past

and was at peace
with that too
as i am now in my house
writing this to you

the house i've fought
my way through to get to

this house which is
not so clean and neat
as yours

      i am a man
i need a woman's touch
might be the pity of it
but i've learned to build
without it
      but now can see
how pleasant such things are
and where they come from
in me
    that is what
i did not know
         and what
i now do know
and will remember

CACTI

I.

love comes
once a month
these days

i am not complaining

it drops on me
unexpectedly
just as rain does
on cactus
in nature
in the desert

it floods me
for a moment
forces new growth
drains away then
in sandy dirt

i am planted
in sandy dirt
insecurely

it is all
a conceit
of course

still
i am not complaining

i am stating
facts of my life
at this moment
and perhaps
from now on

i am
after all
still alive

i have survived
a long time

and i have watched
all the flowering plants
of my life

wither and die
because i did not
handle them
properly
or water them
as they needed
or perhaps
if the new thinking
is correct
did not know
how to talk to them

i am not complaining

i am learning now
that the cactuses
the succulents
even my crown of thorns
continue to grow
to survive
to flourish
without love
or water
more than once
every month

and it has taken
all this time
to learn this
and to learn
that they are my plants
as my life

yet it is true
the kangaroo vine
she left here
is still going
its tendrils reach
out to the lamp
down to the radiator
but this is an aberration
the exception
proving the rule

II.

it is
opuntia rufida
the blind prickly pear
that first declared itself

as if in acknowledgment
of my own blindness
it refused to die
despite the fact
that i expected it to
and perhaps even
out of that expectation
encouraged it to

nevertheless
every time
i left this house
for any length of time
it sent out
new shoots
so that
when i returned
it had children
to greet me

they jutted out
and curved upward
at odd angles
and at odd junctures
from the main body

they were
bright green
even though
rufida itself
tends to blue
or gray green

now this cactus
will even grow
while i am home
and the shoots
continue to be
phallic in nature
just as i myself
have fathered
nothing but sons

cattle relish feeding
on the joints
of opuntia rufida
in the wild
and on its
small fleshy
bright red fruit

which i have never seen
but the plant
is supplied
with glochids
or thin barbed bristles
which fill the areoles
where spines would grow
in other cacti

these glochids
readily penetrate the eye
and blind the cattle
feeding there

next to rufida
there are two cacti
grafted together
as one

at the top
gymnocalycium
asterias
a bright orange globe
with tuberculate ribs
each tubercule swelling
just below the areole
so that the cactus
is called chinned

under it
cereus ocamponis
of which it is said
old stems turn
dull bluish-green
and the rib margins
become brown and horny

mine fits this description
it must be very old

the book also says
gymnocalycium
is self-sterile
in most species
and that hybrids abound
in this genus

next to that pot
on my table

a different variety
of cereus stands

it has just
been given to me
and i do not
understand it yet

it is tall
it is light green
it is shooting
a new growth
straight up
from its top

we watch each other
carefully
we will have to learn
to live with each other

behind this front rank
stand the others

to the left
echinocereus
a hedgehog cactus

it is self-contained
and silent too
as are all cacti
but has attracted
from somewhere
an unnamed succulent
which has sprung up
beside it

the succulent
is very young
but already tall
with small thick leaves

it is ready
for its own pot
but i am afraid
to transplant it

it is not
related to
the jade or

happiness tree
as they call it
in england
which grows
separate and distinct
in its own pot
a handspan away

this succulent
i am told
should have its
leaves wiped clean
every fortnight
but i do not believe
this happens
in nature

new york city
is not nature
and we do
the best we can
in its grime

since it and i
continue to flourish
i credit such happiness
as we have
to this jade
doing its best
in this house

i told you
i am not complaining
at the rear
of all these plants
rearing proudly
is euphorbia
my crown of thorns
which i rescued
from friends who
despaired of it
tired perhaps
of its stance
or its obduracy

having watched
the cacti grow well
i was emboldened
to try this one also
and brought it home

even though then
i did not know
its name

i was born in east virginny
to caroline
where it did go
and there i spied
a fair young maiden
her name and age
i did not know
says the song

this plant
grows tall
with thin green leaves
small sharp thorns
and a woody curving stem

still it is
a succulent
i am told
and it has
a rare
hard
and terrifying beauty
that makes us equal
as we face each other

III.

these plants
enlarge my landscape
and make it green

no this green
is not leafy
or flowering
it is not
the beauty
many depend on
but it does not
leave me
and it gives hope

spikes
spines
thorns
thin barbed bristles
protect it

and when you touch
we hold on

we do not
grab you

you must
come to us
like the rain
once a month
out of nowhere
out of blue
and beautiful
skies that rain
otherwise
on leafy
flowering plants

this is why
i am not complaining

i am learning
how to live

i am learning
i am neither rose
nor weed of the field
but did not know that
and suffered long
trying to be such
trying to grow that way

i am not complaining
i thrive
even though
i grow older

i grow stronger

the only ones
that i hurt
these days
are the ones
who do not understand
and try to
grab me
or come to eat
too ravenously
and are blinded for it
or those

who laugh
to see my
brown and horny
rib margins
my colors of
blue or gray green
and cannot accept
that this
is beauty also
and a way
to keep living
in a hostile
climate
in a soil
that would not
support an ordinary beauty

those who cannot accept
another way
to live

A BEGINNING

we are here
in this place

we hunt these
new beasts

we take their
hides and their furs
to the island
to meet the ships

we were brought
to do this
          in this
new place where
fog covers all
too often

the sun tells us
how the year moves

when the sun rose
in the notch
the priest prepared

for its coming
it was the new year

now it is darker
it is four months later
we watch the sun
dying slowly now

it will die
faster and faster
and the dark will come

we will be alone
in this new place
without the ships
for the winter
building our piles
of furs and hides

we were brought here
for this
      the mother
came with us
her belly filled
by the father

. . . . .

there are others here
with different faces

i have taken one
of their women
and they have taken me

we show each other

what we do

they know
these strange beasts
but i know the mother
and the father
and the coming
of the new year
and they
do not

her skin is a
different color
and the paint
on her face is
different too
and her hair springs
alive under my hand
and is black

I gave myself
to her
    my friend
gave himself back
to the mother

that has never
happened before

he asked the men
on the ships
to take him home
from this fog

they would not

i asked him
to take my woman's
sister
    he could not

he gave himself
back to the mother

he could not
eat the strange things
that grow here

and the bear
of this place
was different
to him
    he was afraid

i saw that this bear
was our bear's brother
and i welcomed him
as he welcomed me

and i eat

the strange things
that my woman
knows how to cook

. . . . .

ah, even the rocks
are different here

still we can build
places to pray

and the mother of mothers
mothers of heroes
the fathers of fathers
who is the sun
of the new year
all have travelled
here with us
in the ships
over the water

and the priests
have come
with the prayers

and we make
our homes here
and there will be
small ones too

to grow big
in this place

where we meet the
ships with our cargo

LESSONS

I

the war was over
                they found helen in
deiphobus' house

               he had taken her
there after paris was killed
                      against her
will

    she had given herself to paris
willingly enough

              deiphobus was
not what she had bargained for

                     so they burst
into the house
          both menelaus and
odysseus
       to kill these two

             but as
graves tells us
        "some say helen herself plunged
a dagger into deiphobus' back"

this and the sight of her naked breasts so
weakened menelaus in his resolve
that "she must die!" he threw away his sword
and led her in safety back to the ships

II

the point isn't
that he fought that war
or vowed that she must die

it isn't even that
they left together
spent the exile in egypt
went home to sparta
together

                it is that
moment
            and the dreams
that led to it

the dreams you have
when someone
leaves you for
another
            and when
they are beautiful
in your eyes and
the other's and
the world's eyes too

so he raised his kinsmen
and their armies
and he fought
to kill her
and avenge his honor

the sight of
her naked breasts
ended this war

all through that war
he must have had
this certain dream
every little once in a while

this dream in which
he finds himself
again and again

he is bringing gifts
—beware a greek
bringing gifts—
yet bringing gifts
to her
        to ask
forgiveness
            since
we do decide we are
the one who's wrong

we ask forgiveness
in our dreams

while wide awake
we know how
wronged we are

in our dreams
we beg acceptance
and a smile

oh yes we know
that we have wronged

why else be alone
alone we hope
to be forgiven
having done that wrong

in this certain dream
helen sits waiting

we open the gift
for her
      it
astounds her
and she smiles
then laughs

we smile and laugh
as she accepts it
thus accepting us

so good in the dream
we wake sick with anger
having dreamed it

real anger that
somewhere deep
we still suck around
still beg

      even
menelaus
      for helen's
naked breasts
her smile
and all

even when we know

            the loss and time
gone
      know that
it's over
         dead

we want it that way

at the same time
we want that love
just as it used to be

we want those
buttermilk breasts
that perfect face
that acceptance
the tender love
she had once felt
for us we thought

even knowing all this time
she deserves her paris
and he her
            perfect for
each other
         as we had
thought that we were perfect
once

     even for the world
they are the perfect
couple coupled

yet we cry why
paris why him why
her
   where did i
go wrong

SPRING

this letter
is long overdue

it was promised
in february
and now it is
late in spring

february because
it is on the second
of that month
that persephone
begins her journey
up to earth

but the letter
is not for her
but for her lover dis
who as lawrence tells us
sends that spring
chasing at her heels

she flees his dark house
and he sends flowers
snapping at her heels

friends glorying in spring
in the country
mistake me also
and send letters
to tell each glimmering
change of season
as if it did not happen here

so the letter is
in a different sense
for them also
to announce we know it here
as well
        that spring
comes just as surely
every time it should

i announce spring
therefore
        in the city

flowers on bethune street
and on bank
        in little
plots of earth exposed
around the trees that
stalk the sidewalks

snowdrops first as usual
then croci now tulips
daffodils and where space
is wider cherry trees

others have pictured
this place differently
they feel sorry for us
locked
     but dis knows
cities too
       the flowers
come snapping at her heels
even here
        so

i announce spring

FIVE ATTEMPTS AT THE ARMENIAN

TARGET SHOOTING

Aim straight at the bull's eye
and you will always miss
    no door will open
    no doll fall down
    not a single bird will topple
all of them will stand proudly
staring at you.

Forget the goal, don't worry about aimimg,
fire the gun left and right, up and down,
    the doors will open
    the dolls will fall in your lap
    oh the roasted birds into your mouth—
and you will be a marksman.

                Zareh Kharakkouni *(born 1926)*

GIVE ME MY EYES

an excerpt from a longer poem

Give me my hands
and I'll get colored lights for you
and one by one the whisper of flowers.
I'll catch sound in mid-air,
I'll squeeze sea-water in my palm
and sprinkle salt on your flat food.
With those hands I'll pull sound out of my lips
and diamonds out of the wind.

Give me my eyes
so that I can see you just as you're made.
Don't let me be blind: Give me back my eyes!
Let me look at compassion with compassion.

Give me my heart—
instead of a heart I have a tired, worn-out creature.
I keep dragging it with me, it keeps dragging me with it,
and we drag each other down unknown streets.
Give me my heart
and I'll take away your pain,
I'll squeeze the sorrow out of your eyes,
I'll fill your soul with lights, with joy.

Give me my lips
and with them I'll pick flowers from the earth.
I'll kiss a rock, it will become a church.
I'll kiss your eyes, your lips, your voices,
I'll kiss the silence
and it will tell you stories.
I'll kiss colors and they'll brim with tears
and they will mix with the shivers of happiness
and we will all get lost in them.

Give me my lips
and I'll sing a holy mass for you
and pray for you
and the arches of this church will touch the sky . . .

Razmik Davoyan *(born 1940)*

FOR HASMIK

When these days aren't any more,
and I'm gone like a dream,
I'll come in through your wet eyes
when you don't expect it.

At that hopeless moment
you'll open the door to memory
and your divine fingers will start to tremble—
your lovers will tremble between those fingers—
over the memories unlost, but not yet found.

You will bend gently over my lines
as forgotten memoirs are read;
pushing aside thoughts and years
you will sigh a thousand times
like waves breaking and breaking.

My voice will bring back my image
and it will appear before you a mirage—
clean of all thoughts, all filth, the world—
Hasmik . . . Hasmik . . . Hasmik . . .

My voice will echo through your nerves
and I'll sink into your breast
where I'll stay forever,
like a lover, like a dead man,
I'll be sleeping there.

And no trouble, no storm
will tear me out of your ribs.
Together we'll pass through this sad world
like wind, detached from myths.

Razmik Davoyan *(born 1940)*

WE WERE WALKING

We walked in the fields.
The trees were new planted
and the sky was high and bright.
A young wind played with her hair.

She asked questions. Life
was the problem for us both.
Her eyes shone like olives.

Suddenly she ran from me
to pick some flowers.

I sat on a stone. She came back
to throw the flowers on my knees
and put her shoulder next to mine.

She smelled of violets
and fresh sweat.

Costan Zarian *(1885-1969)*

THE OWL

In the grey night, again, the endless row
of cypress trees. Always that same black line.
Silent terror: the stars' eternal glow
lost behind the clouds, which also cloud the moon.

The dark trees soar together in one flight
toward their vision of another place
beyond this grey, repeated, faithful night.
the trees are just as faithful in their race.

Let my world's passions calm themselves as well—
let all driving thoughts stay silent and unsaid—
so that my silent dream touches Heaven's bell.

But suddenly an owl screams piercing red.
Alas! It is the same within my self
when some sharp eye wakes in my darkened head.

Diran Chrakian (Indra) *(1875-1921)*

FOR MAX

phones and trucks
all the trappings
this modern life
and he is gone

old-young young-old
no longer here

in the middle of
progress always
looking the other way

met and touched
gave took talked
and always talked
and he is gone

hungry on
the orient express
the eyes to see
the ears all
ears
    and gone now
from all of this

THE OLDEST

mother
was stone

teeth bit

sisters none
i longed

two wives
no longer

never daughters

now one
i flower

loving him
same mystery

we share that

BIBLIOGRAPHY

The Dancer. Jargon 2. Black Mountain, N.C.: (Jonathan Williams), 1951. Broadside.

Four Poems to Spring. Black Mountain, N.C.: Published by the author, 1951.

The Dutiful Son. Jargon 16. (Highlands, N.C.): Jonathan Williams, 1956.

The Love Bit, and Other Poems. New York: Totem Press in association with Corinth Books, 1962.

The Great American Desert. Evergreen Playscript no. 3. New York: Grove Press, 1966.

A Treatise. New York: Brownstone Press, 1966.

Sirventes on a Sad Occurrence. Madison, Wis.: Perishable Press, 1967.

When the Drums Stopped. Pleasant Valley, N.Y.: Krija Press of Sri Ram Ashrama, 1967. Broadside.

In Time: Poems 1962-1968. Indianapolis and New York: Bobbs-Merrill, 1969.

17-18 April, 1961. Press of the Black Flag Raised no. 5. [Somerville, Mass.]: Press of the Black Flag Raised, [1970]. Broadside.

On Occasion: Some Births, Deaths, Weddings, Birthdays, Holidays, and Other Events. Indianapolis and New York: Bobbs-Merrill, 1973.

The Wrong Season. Introduction by Joe Flaherty. Indianapolis and New York: Bobbs-Merrill, 1973. Cloth edition. A paper edition was published by Award Books, New York, in 1974. Prose.

Pan's Eyes. A Haystack Book. Amherst, Mass.: Mulch Press, 1974. Short stories.

The Lesson; Art; Hyacinths; Nature. Kent, Ohio: Kent State University, 1974. Broadside.

The Woman Poems. Indianapolis: Bobbs-Merrill, 1975.

Acts. Driftless, Wisc.: The Perishable Press, 1976.

Names, Dates and Places. Laurinburg, N.C.: St. Andrews Press, 1978.

It is Such. Buffalo, N.Y.: Friends of the University Libraries, University of Buffalo, 1979. Broadside.

Chai Number One. Gloucester, Mass.: Bezoar, 1979.

On the Giving of a Talas. New York: Privately printed, 1979. Broadside.

Just Friends/Friends and Lovers: Poems 1959-1962. Jargon 57. Highland, N.C.: Jargon Press, 1980.

The Only Anarchist General. Rocky Mount, N.C.: Arthur Mann Kaye, 1980. Broadside.

Houses. Buffalo, N.Y.: White Pine Press, 1981.

Marilyn Lives!. New York: Delilah Books, 1981. prose.

The Progression Begins. New York: #Magazine, 1981.

Del Quien Lo Tomo: A Suite. Minor Confluence, U.S.A.: Perishable Press Limited, 1982.

At Fifty. Laurinburg, N.C.: St. Andrews Press, 1982.

2 From At Fifty. Rocky Mount, N.C.: Arthur Mann Kaye, 1982. Broadside.

The Ghost Lover. Rocky Mount, N.C.: Arthur Mann Kaye, 1983.

Poetry, the Ecology of the Soul: Talks and Selected Poems. Buffalo, N.Y.: White Pine Press, 1983.